PITTSBURGH
ON YOUR PLATE!

A Collection of Recipes and Stories about Pittsburgh

JOANNE NIEHL

First Edition

PAGE PUBLISHING, INC.
Conneaut Lake, PA

First originally published by Page Publishing 2020

ISBN 978-1-64701-506-0 (pbk)
ISBN 978-1-64701-507-7 (digital)

Printed in the United States of America

To the loves of my life
My husband, Les
My children
Jacob, Adam, and Julia

You all make me the person I am.
Forever in my heart!

CONTENTS

FOREWORD

Julia Child, Gordon Ramsay, that Jiro fella from the sushi movie—all are great chefs of history, but none of the three gave birth to us, so someone else had to write the forewords to their books. Additionally, we weren't raised by their cooking. The recipes in their books didn't make us feel better when we were sick or teach us how to take care of ourselves when we were ready to leave the house. We've been bragging about this cooking for almost thirty years, and now, finally, here it is in physical-book form.

They say it takes ten thousand hours to become an expert in something. By that standard, you could say that we are extensively studied experts in our mom's cooking, multiple times over. As such, we are qualified to tell you that the recipes in this book have been thoroughly tested (by Julia in the cooking department, with Adam and Jake leading the consumption wing) and approved to be authentically Pittsburgh in both taste and in nature.

Every dish in this book comes from a place of love and family but also from a place of thick Pittsburghese accents and closets half composed of black and gold clothing. The greater Pittsburgh area is almost as important a member of our family as any one of us Niehls, so it only makes sense that it plays such a vital role in this cookbook. Joanne has spent decades in Pittsburgh, constantly bettering her cooking skills, learning from and teaching those lucky enough to have spent time in the kitchen with her, and now she's offering her helping hand to you, reader.

Tie up your apron, and roll up your sleeves. It's time to cook like a Yinzer.

Juli, Adam, and Jake Niehl

PREFACE

Pittsburgh is a place of great families and great food. I have tried throughout these pages to give the reader a glimpse into the experiences in my personal life as well as my journey to becoming a good home cook. I want you, the reader, to sense the recipe. Think of where it came from, who made it, and who enjoyed it. I didn't want to produce a book with just recipe after recipe. I wanted you to step into my world—my Pittsburgh world. I have always been fascinated with the ethnicity of the Pittsburgh area, and I hope that shines through these pages.

My mom's Italian family (Capezzuto) and my dad's Irish family (Lutton) formed the basis of the ethnic foods that I was exposed to growing up. But I can also still see the Croatian ladies two houses up the street from mine, gathered around a table as they stretched the dough to make their strudel. I was amazed at the size of the dough when they were finished. I loved how they talked in Croatian and laughed but kept to their work. And then, of course, the smell of that strudel baking etched an indelible sensory memory in my mind. I was only seven years old. It was magical, and it was Pittsburgh.

I am so very proud of the Pittsburgh that I know. The humor is sincere. I love the quirkiness. Oh, the quirkiness! The personality of Pittsburgh is so apparent in the way we talk, the food we eat, the traditions we preserve, and the things we hold dear. We are all different, but at the same time, we are all the same. If I can convey this through the journey of foods, then my efforts will be fulfilled.

I have tried to include recipes that relate to the people I have met. It is a learning journey. I always listen especially closely when someone is describing how something is made and they say, "My grandma used to…" My ears perk up immediately! That is the important stuff. The precious little details—like Mike Bujakowski's mom, Adelia, adding applesauce to her stuffed cabbage—are the culinary diamonds in the rough that I love. She learned it from her Polish mother and grandmother. That's the way to make it!

My favorite recipe of all time comes from my wonderful great-grandmother Mariantonetta DeFalco Capezzuto. Her recipe for pasta e fajioli is listed in glasses of water, not cups. And she noted, "Put that glass on the stove, and let it sit while the soup cooks." When I make that recipe, I know we are together. It is the way she made it, and I am honored to do the same.

So I am inviting you to take a Pittsburgh journey with me through the recipes in this book. Think of your own food journey, and savor the memories in your life. If you smile at an anecdote or enjoy one of the recipes and it brings back a good remembrance, that's great! The world is a better place with food and laughter!

PITTSBURGH: THE HEART OF THE CITY

Pittsburgh is a very unique city and area. It is an old soul founded in 1758 by George Washington and General John Forbes. The name Pittsburgh was formulated for the Great Commoner, British prime minister William Pitt. It is an area that has been forged by the common man, hard workers, mostly in the steel industry, hence its nickname, the Steel City. It is the home to more than 300 steel-related businesses. It is also a city of bridges, boasting over 445 of them that span rivers, streams, valleys, and highways. The relatively small city is located between the Monogahela and Allegheny Rivers, which, at their confluence, form the Ohio River. The very point where the rivers merge is celebrated with a spectacular fountain and the surrounding Point State Park. Many of the festivals and celebrations in Pittsburgh happen in Point State Park.

The Pittsburgh metropolitan area jumped into the twenty-first century as home to numerous prestigious schools, cutting-edge health-care systems, and high-tech businesses. Home to 68 colleges and universities within shouting distance of downtown and nationally ranked hospital systems, it has become the sixth-best area in the United States for job growth. Pittsburgh has been listed among the most livable cities in the United States in several recent years.

When it comes to food, Pittsburgh was voted the Food City of the Year in 2019. It offers an amazing variety of cuisines. The Western Pennsylvania area has an extensive farm-to-table industry. It allows for the quality that is ever so important to the diversity of the growing local food industry. It is a bourgeoning industry with many pop-up eateries and distinctive culinary establishments and even boasts a restaurant that was listed as one of the ten best restaurants in the world.

The people of Pittsburgh are a very distinctive group. First and foremost, Pittsburghers are a proud people. They are known for their hard-work ethics, their friendliness, and their dialect and unique colloquialisms. But most of all, the people of Pittsburgh are known for their traditions. Many of those traditions are foods and recipes that are carried and inherited through the years. Recipes written in Italian, Slovak, Greek, Polish, Russian, and others define family lifestyles. Certain foods are mandates for specific holidays. The Western Pennsylvania area is well-known for their cookie tables offered at weddings. Cookies are made duteously by relatives, neighbors, and friends and often number in the thousands in the elaborate displays on reception hall tables. It is done with pride and honor and, in many cases, the utmost respect for what came before them.

This cookbook is filled with recipes I have collected throughout the years. Many are from my Italian family, my husband's German family, and just the foods that you cook in Pittsburgh. We are all part of Pittsburgh. We carry that with us every day, no matter where our lives take us. Pittsburgh is in our hearts, and we all know that we were raised Pittsburgh and will always be Pittsburgh.

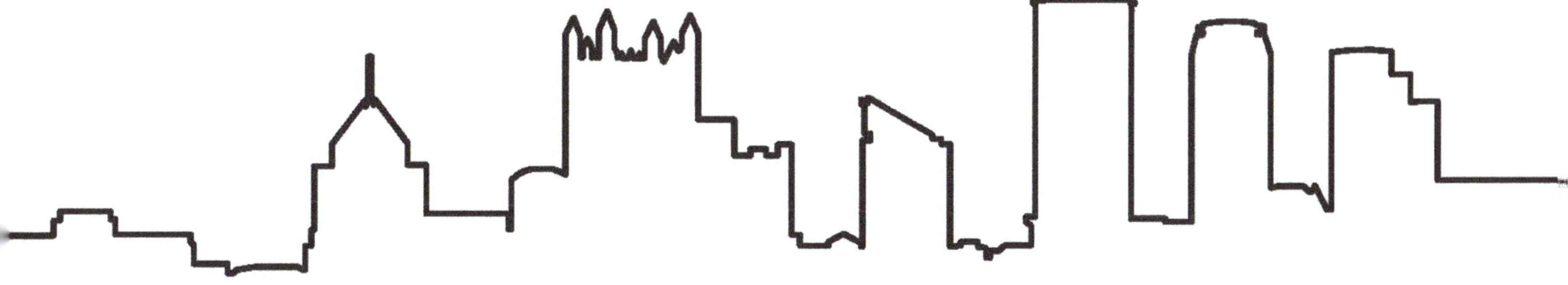

APPETIZERS

AMISH PEANUT BUTTER DIP

Once you taste this dip, you'll love it. And once you make the dip and realize how easy it is to put together, you'll adore it! My Amish friend Lynn Palmer from Lancaster, Pennsylvania, helped me make this recipe possible. Okay, okay, she's really not Amish, but she is from Lancaster! I have kidded her with this for years until I found in my genealogy that one of my grandmothers in the early 1800s was actually Amish. The joke was obviously on me!

INGREDIENTS

16 ounces of marshmallow cream
8 ounces of peanut butter
3 tablespoons light corn syrup
1/4 cup hot water
1 tablespoon maple flavoring

DIRECTIONS

Combine all ingredients in a mixing bowl. With a stand mixer or hand mixer, mix on medium for 5 minutes. Scrape the bowl periodically.

Place the dip in a decorative bowl or container, and keep refrigerated until ready to use. Refrigerate remaining dip for future enjoyment.

Serve with vanilla wafers, cookies, or crackers of your choice.

ANTIPASTO PLATTER

Make a salad an event! An Italian antipasto is perfect for a light lunch or the start to a great dinner meal. Great for a crowd!

INGREDIENTS

Main ingredients:

1 pound assorted deli meats (salami, prosciutto, capicola)
1 pound assorted cheese (mozzarella, provolone, Asiago, blue cheese)
assorted Italian olives
marinated artichoke hearts
1 jar of roasted red peppers cut into strips or fresh made peppers
cherry tomatoes
1 large bunch of lettuce, chopped or torn

For the dressing:

1/2 cup olive oil
1/4 cup red wine vinegar
kosher salt and fresh ground black pepper
fresh basil
fresh Italian bread

DIRECTIONS

Arrange the lettuce as a bed on the platter. Arrange the meats, cheeses, olives, and vegetables atop the lettuce.

Drizzle with dressing. Sprinkle with kosher salt and pepper and fresh basil.

Additional dressing can be used to taste. Always use the formula of twice the olive oil to the red wine vinegar.

Serve with fresh Italian bread or Focaccia bread.

BASIC BRUSCHETTA

Add this with a nice charcuterie or a heaping antipasto, and life is good! A glass of wine with friends and a glowing sunset completes a fun, relaxing start to a great meal.

INGREDIENTS

3 large tomatoes, seeded and chopped
3 tablespoons fresh parsley, chopped
1 tablespoon fresh chives, chopped
2 tablespoons fresh basil, chopped
2 cloves garlic, minced
1/3 cup olive oil
salt and pepper to taste
French baguette, sliced and toasted or grilled

DIRECTIONS

Mix all ingredients except the baguette, and refrigerate for 1–2 hours.
Place a tablespoon on each baguette slice.
Arrange on a platter, and serve.
To serve warm, shaved Parmesan or mozzarella cheese can be added to this bruschetta.
Top with the selected cheese, and allow to heat in a 350-degree oven for 10 minutes. And then serve.

CHEDDAR PUFFS

My husband, Les, who is totally German, calls these cream puffs with cheese. The man truly will eat anything I serve him. He is always complimentary and willing to help in any endeavor I think of, and trust me, there have been quite a few! I may have pushed the envelope when I brought home a rescue chicken, who lived on our deck for twelve years. But oh, the wonderful fresh eggs!

INGREDIENTS

1/2 cup butter
2 cups sharp cheddar cheese, grated
dash of salt
1 teaspoon smoky paprika
dash cayenne or more if you like it hot
1 cup sifted flour
50 (approx.) green olives

DIRECTIONS

Blend softened butter with cheese, salt, paprika, and cayenne.
Mix in the flour.
Form balls around the olives, and place on baking sheet.
Chill until firm.
Bake at 350 degrees for 25 minutes.
Serve warm.

CHICKEN, PEAR, GORGONZOLA TARTS

This appetizer is quick, easy and looks like you made a great effort to prepare it!

INGREDIENTS

- 10 slices peppered bacon
- 2 tablespoons brown sugar
- 1/4 teaspoon cinnamon
- 1 cup chicken, cooked and chopped
- 1/3 cup pear nectar or juice
- 2 packages frozen mini phyllo tart shells
- 1/4 cup apricot preserves
- 1/3 cup pears, finely chopped
- 2 tablespoons butter
- 1/3 cup gorgonzola cheese

DIRECTIONS

Sprinkle the bacon with the brown sugar, and fry. When fully cooked and crispy, drain and crumble the bacon.

Combine the chicken, pears, pear nectar, apricot preserves, butter, cinnamon, salt, and pepper in a saucepan.

Bring the mixture to a boil, and allow to cook for 3 to 4 minutes.

Spoon into the tarts and top with the crumbled bacon and gorgonzola cheese.

Bake filled tarts at 350 degrees for 5 to 7 minutes.

CHIPOTLE SHRIMP SKEWERS

Shrimp on skewers is always a great idea. If you are using wooden skewers, let them soak in water for an hour before you use them so they won't catch on fire.

INGREDIENTS

1/2 cup chipotle barbeque sauce
1 tablespoon lime juice
2 cloves garlic, crushed
24 extra large shrimp, cleaned, with tails
48 fresh pineapple cubes
24 mini bamboo appetizer skewers

DIRECTIONS

Combine the chipotle sauce, lime juice, and garlic, and place in a bowl or ziplock bag. Add the cleaned shrimp and pineapple.

Allow to marinate for 2–4 hours.

Using the small skewers, place a cube of pineapple, then a shrimp, and end with another pineapple cube.

Grill until the shrimp are cooked.

This recipe could be made with cubes of chicken as well.

Serve warm.

CRAB PUFFS

These may require a little more effort, but they are such a nice addition to your appetizers.

INGREDIENTS

4 ounces imitation crab, broken into small pieces
3 ounces cream cheese, softened
1/8 teaspoon garlic salt
1/8 teaspoon Worcestershire sauce
1/2 teaspoon sugar
1 green onion, finely chopped
14 wonton wrappers

DIRECTIONS

Mix all the ingredients together. Take each wonton wrapper, and brush all the sides with water. Place a teaspoon of the crab mix in the center of the wrapper.

Fold bottom point to the top, forming a triangle. Press along the edges to seal. Brush the sides of the triangle with water and bring each bottom edge to the top point. Press to seal.

Deep-fry until golden brown.

CURRIED CHICKEN-STUFFED CHERRY TOMATOES

These are a little labor-intensive, but in the midst of the summer, when the sweet tomatoes are so ripe, it's a nice appetizer. Leftover stuffing can be enjoyed on crackers!

INGREDIENTS

1 pint cherry tomatoes (about 25 pieces)
3–4 cooked chicken breasts
1 cup almonds, toasted
1 large apple, peeled and cored
2 teaspoon chopped onion
1 teaspoon curry powder
1 cup mayonnaise (mayo and a tangy dressing)

DIRECTIONS

Remove the tops, and hollow the tomatoes. Invert on a rack or paper towels to allow the tomatoes to drain.

In a food processor, pulse the chicken, almonds, apple, and onion. Pulse the food processor until a coarse mix is made.

Blend together the curry powder and mayonnaise, and add to the chicken mixture.

Pipe or spoon the mixture into each cherry tomato.

Chill and serve.

FILLED STRAWBERRIES

This is a lovely addition to a summer platter. Strawberries are one of the most common fruits grown in the Pittsburgh area. Many local farms offer pick-your-own strawberries, which provides for a fun family outing! We have grown strawberries in our yard for years and, at times, will have tiny strawberries growing in the lawn along with the grass!

INGREDIENTS

1–2 quarts medium to large strawberries, washed
6 ounces cream cheese, room temperature
1/2 teaspoon vanilla
2 tablespoon powdered sugar

DIRECTIONS

Trim the bottom of each strawberry flat to allow the berry to stand securely. Cut off the very top of the berry, and scoop out the inside. Allow to sit and dry before filling.

Whip the cream cheese for 2 to 3 minutes. Add the vanilla and the powdered sugar, and continue to beat until smooth and creamy.

Place the filling in a pastry bag with a star tip. Overfill each strawberry. A toasted almond can be placed in the top of each.

Refrigerate.

GRACE'S SPINACH PIE

This spinach pie is a specialty of my friend Grace McGhee. She is a remarkable person. She is a very astute businesswoman as well as a world traveler and has an amazing knowledge of all things, including cooking. She has been a friend of mine since the seventh grade, and no matter where our lives have led us, we have always stayed in touch. We just pick up where we left off and move on through life. Everyone could use a friend like Grace.

INGREDIENTS

1/4 cup oil
1 1/4 medium onions, chopped
2 10-ounce packages frozen spinach
4 eggs, beaten
1 pound cottage cheese
1/2 pound feta cheese, crumbled
1/4 pound Fontinella cheese, coarsely grated
1/2 pound unsalted butter
1 package phyllo dough

DIRECTIONS

Defrost and drain spinach.

Sauté onions in the oil until golden. Add the spinach to the skillet, and simmer for 5–6 minutes. Remove from the heat, and set aside.

In a separate bowl, add the eggs and beat. Add the cheeses to the beaten eggs. Stir together, and add to the cooked spinach. Set aside.

Butter a large 13-by-9-inch pan. Place 9 sheets of phyllo in the pan, and brush each with melted butter. Pour the spinach mixture over the phyllo, and cover with another 9 sheets of phyllo, brushing butter on each sheet.

Refrigerate for several hours. Cut the pie into squares, and sprinkle with water to prevent the sheets from curling.

Bake in a 350-degree oven for 45 minutes or until browned.

MY FAVORITE NIECE'S CRAB DIP (JEAN KUKLEWSKI)

Jean is the mathematician of the family—such a sweet person! She is always so assuring as well as calm and collected.

INGREDIENTS

- 11 ounces cream cheese, softened
- 1 small onion, minced
- 5 tablespoons mayonnaise
- 12 ounces crabmeat, drained and flaked
- 1/8 teaspoon garlic powder
- salt and pepper to taste
- 1 pound loaf of bread or crackers

DIRECTIONS

Combine all ingredients except the crackers or loaf of bread and spread into a one-quart baking dish.
Bake in a 350-degree oven for 20 minutes.
Serve hot on crackers or bread.

MY FAVORITE NIECE'S DEVILED EGGS (JEAN KUKLEWSKI)

Jean is also an engineer! She tutors students with such patience. She once told me how rewarding it is when a student finally understands, like a light bulb goes on. I assured her that if she were to tutor me in math, we would probably have to resort to a candle!

INGREDIENTS

12 hard-boiled eggs
2 teaspoons vinegar
2 teaspoons prepared mustard
1/2 cup mayonnaise
1/8 teaspoon salt

DIRECTIONS

Peel hard-boiled eggs, and cut each lengthwise. Carefully remove the egg yolks, and mash.
Mix the remaining ingredients with the mashed yolks to form a smooth paste.
Fill each egg half with the yolk mixture, using a spoon or piping bag.
Keep refrigerated.
Sprinkle with paprika, and serve cold.

PINEAPPLE CHEESE BALL

Les's mom, Matilda Sholder Niehl, used this recipe for her card club. Many Pittsburghers played cards weekly, usually their game of choice was pinochle or 500 bid. Les always loved when it was his mom's turn to host. The snacks were on each table, and the bridge mix was his favorite. He would pick out all the chocolate-covered peanuts and raisins!

INGREDIENTS

2–8 ounces cream cheese, softened
1 small can pineapple, drained
1 tablespoon onion, minced
1/4 cup green pepper, finely chopped
2 tablespoons parsley, chopped
1 tablespoon seasoned salt
2 cups pecans, toasted and chopped

DIRECTIONS

Mix all ingredients except the pecans.
Form into a ball, and roll in the pecans.
Refrigerate until set.
Serve with crackers.

SPINACH LOAF

This is a nice appetizer or even a nice complement to a charcuterie platter. It is tasty warm and at room temperature.

INGREDIENTS

1 cup cooked rice
1 cup celery, including leaves, chopped
1/2 pound loose pork sausage, cooked
1 box frozen chopped spinach, cooked and drained
1 medium onion, minced
3 eggs
1 teaspoon salt
1 teaspoon pepper
grated cheese

DIRECTIONS

Mix all ingredients in the order given, and form into a loaf.
Place in butter casserole, and cover with cheese.
Bake at 350 degrees for 30 minutes.

SWEET CORN GUACAMOLE

This recipe is from our daughter, Juli. We had never eaten guacamole until about three years ago. Now we are hooked! This has such a rich goodness and is heaven on a tortilla chip!

INGREDIENTS

4 fresh avocados (choose ones that are soft to touch)
1 red bell pepper
2 cups sweet corn
1 tablespoon lime juice
1 cup salsa
salt and pepper to taste

DIRECTIONS

Slice avocado in two, and remove pit. Scoop out avocado flesh.
Place all ingredients in food processor, and process until smooth.
Chill and serve with tortilla chips.

PITTSBURGH SPORTS

Pittsburgh is known worldwide for its sports teams. We are the City of Champions, the only city in the United States where all three of the major league sports teams share the same colors. Thus, we are often known simply as the Black and Gold. Superbowls, Stanley Cups, and World Series—we have enjoyed them all multiple times. And we expect them in the future—every year, as a matter of fact. People here say they bleed black and gold. I have come to believe that is a true statement. Last week, I read an obituary of a man who requested all those attending his funeral to wear black and gold. To say it runs deep is an understatement. But it's good, very good! It is the glue that makes the people of Pittsburgh all brothers and sisters. We all bleed black and gold to some extent.

When I was a kid, every once in a great while, my dad, Howard, would take me to a Pirate baseball game, one time even at the venerable old Forbes Field. It was a great day when we would go see the Pirates. At one game, they were giving out Green Weenies. This plastic green wiener that really resembled a green pickle was filled with beans. When the opposing team came to bat, the crowd shook their Green Weenies at the batter, giving him the bad eye! Not sure it worked. But many years later, Les and I and friends went to a game, and there behind us sat a lady with her very old Green Weenie! It was in great shape, and she shook it during the entire game. Around the seventh inning, a guy sitting three seats over had had enough. He yelled loudly, "OKAY! OKAY! ENOUGH WITH THE GREEN WEENIE!" There was total silence. We all just sat quietly, biting our lips and holding back laughter. After only two or three minutes of silence, we heard "Shoup-shoup-shoup!" She went right back to her endless shaking. We looked at one another and laughed uproariously, then sat back and enjoyed the rest of the game. It's Pittsburgh! That lady was there with her forty-year-old Green Weenie, and damn if she wasn't going to make the best of it!

The Pirates may not be a winning team, but they certainly are a wonderful host for all Pittsburghers. The food offered at the stadium is amazing. There are always cool giveaways, and in every game, there is a pierogi Race with four people dressed in pierogi suits racing around the entire perimeter of the field. Who doesn't love someone running a race in a pierogi suit!

It's just so Pittsburgh!

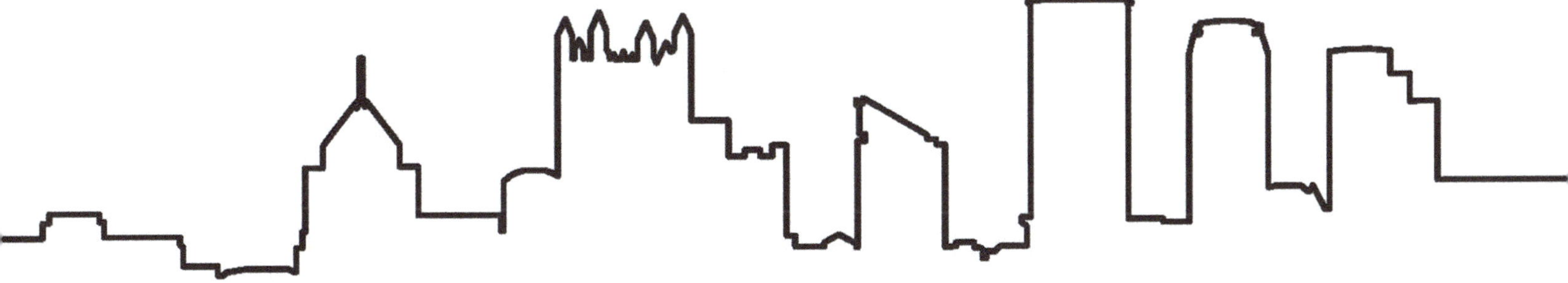

SOUPS AND BREADS

ANDOUILLE-SAUSAGE-AND-SHRIMP CREAM SOUP

This recipe can be altered to your level of spicy heat. You can change the andouille sausage to Italian sausage, and lessen or increase the amount of jalapeño pepper and cayenne.

INGREDIENTS

1/2 pound cooked andouille sausage, cut into thin slices
1 medium onion, chopped
2 celery ribs, chopped
1 medium red pepper, chopped
1 medium green pepper, chopped
1 jalapeño pepper, seeded and chopped
1/4 cup butter
3 cloves garlic, chopped
2 cups white sweet corn
4 medium Roma tomatoes, chopped
1 cup chicken broth
1 teaspoon chili powder
1/2 teaspoon salt
1/2 teaspoon pepper
1 pound medium uncooked shrimp, peeled and deveined
1 cup heavy cream
1/2 teaspoon cayenne (or more to taste)

DIRECTIONS

Sauté the first 6 ingredients in butter until tender.
Add garlic, and cook for 1 minute more.
Add the tomatoes, broth, corn, and spices and bring to a boil. Reduce heat, and simmer for 10 minutes.
Stir in the shrimp and heavy cream, and bring to a boil.
Simmer 10 minutes or until the shrimp turns pink.

APPLESAUCE PUMPKIN BREAD

This is a moist tasty bread that is great with a cup of coffee or tea. It's very easy to make, and it freezes so well! It goes perfectly on an autumn morning with glowing leaves drifting in the gentle breeze.

INGREDIENTS

2/3 cup butter
2–2/3 cup sugar
4 eggs
1 cup applesauce
1 cup canned pumpkin
3–1/3 cup flour
2 teaspoons baking soda
1/2 teaspoon baking powder
1 1/2 teaspoons salt
1 teaspoon cinnamon
1/2 teaspoon nutmeg
2/3 cup apple juice
1 cup chopped walnuts

DIRECTIONS

Cream the butter and sugar together.

Add eggs one at a time, allowing each to be beaten well into the mix.

Stir in the applesauce and pumpkin.

In a separate bowl, sift together all the dry ingredients. Stir the dry ingredients alternatively with the apple juice into the applesauce-pumpkin mixture. Stir until just incorporated and moist. Lastly, stir in the nuts.

Pour batter into two greased loaf pans.

Bake at 350 degrees for 1 hour. Test doneness by inserting a toothpick or cake tester. When it comes out clean, the bread is done.

Allow loaves to cool, and then remove it from pan. Enjoy now or freeze for later.

BULK PIZZA DOUGH

This is my beloved Aunt Julie's recipe. I called her ZiaZia. She loved to sing opera. She was quite the soprano. Despite being Italian, we did not have pizza often, but when she made it, it was on a large cookie sheet, always square and always with pepperoni and cheese, and Uncle Tony would go down to the fruit cellar for the wine… Dago red, of course!

INGREDIENTS

1 large cake of yeast
3/4 cup warm water
1 teaspoon sugar
1 tablespoon salt
3 tablespoon oil
3 cups warm water
9 cups flour

DIRECTIONS

Dissolve yeast in 3/4 cup of warm water and sugar. Allow to proof.

Mix the flour and salt, and make a well in the center. Add the proofed yeast, water, and oil, and form a dough. Knead well, and allow to rise until it doubles in size. Roll out enough dough for pan or stone.

Top with your favorite sauce, cheese, and toppings, and bake at 425 degrees until the crust is brown and the toppings are hot.

These pizza shells can be baked (at 425 degrees for 10–12 minutes) and frozen for future use.

CATHY'S FAMOUS PICNIC BUNS

My sister-in-law, Cathy May, is known for these buns. My parents, Howard and Angie Lutton, would rave for days about them. On holidays, Cathy always had warm rolls waiting for my parents when they walked in the door. I used to tell her she was getting my share of the inheritance based on those damn rolls. Joking aside, they are a good bake.

INGREDIENTS

2 cups warm water (110 degrees)
2 packages dry yeast or 1 compressed yeast
1/2 cup sugar
2 teaspoons salt
1/4 cup shortening, softened
1 egg, beaten
6–7 cups flour, sifted

DIRECTIONS

Place warm water and yeast in bowl, and allow to proof. Stir in sugar, salt, softened shortening, and beaten egg. Add enough flour to make the dough workable. Turn dough onto a floured board, and knead until smooth and elastic. Place in greased bowl, and allow to rise until doubled in size (for 1 1/2 hours). When doubled, punch down again, and allow to rise again for 30 minutes until almost doubled.

Cut the dough, and shape it into buns. Place them on lightly greased cookie sheet, and allow to rise for 30–45 minutes.

Bake in a 400-degree oven for 12–15 minutes or until golden brown.

This makes 3 dozen buns.

CREAM-OF-GARLIC SOUP

An Italian favorite! This soup takes form at the very last when you blend the ingredients and the very soft potatoes form a creamy soup base. Believe it or not, the garlic is not overwhelming.

INGREDIENTS

20 bulbs of garlic (not heads, but individual bulbs)
1/4 cup butter
1 onion, chopped
1 large scallion, chopped
2 cups chicken stock
5 medium potatoes, peeled and diced into small pieces
2 cups milk or cream
1 tablespoon Italian flat parsley
salt and pepper to taste

DIRECTIONS

Take the 20 garlic bulbs in their jackets, and allow to sit in hot water for 10 to 15 minutes. When they are cool to the touch, remove skins.

In a soup pot, melt butter and sauté the onions and scallion until transparent. Add the garlic bulbs. Allow to cook until soft.

Add the chicken stock. Add the potatoes, cream and parsley. Allow this to cook for at least 40 minutes. The potatoes should be soft.

Before serving, using a handheld blender, pulse the mix until it is smooth.

Add salt and pepper to taste, and serve.

DATE-AND-NUT BREAD

Many Christmas cookie platters will include a variety of breads including nut, date, apple, and pumpkin. These breads are often accompanied with butter or cream cheese. They are easy to make, and they go well with coffee or tea. Our Italian Christmases not only offered these, but there was always a platter of dried fruits and a wooden bowl of shelled nuts.

INGREDIENTS

1 pound chopped dates
2 cups boiling water
3 teaspoons baking soda
1/4 cup butter
1 3/4 cup sugar
3 eggs
3 1/2 cups flour
1 1/2 cups chopped walnuts
1 teaspoon vanilla

DIRECTIONS

Boil the 2 cups water, and add the 3 teaspoons baking soda. Pour this mixture over the chopped dates, and let stand for 30 to 45 minutes. Drain and set aside.

Stir all the ingredients, including the dates, together until well mixed. Place in two greased small loaf pans.

Bake at 325 degrees for 1 hour or until done, testing for doneness when an inserted toothpick is clean when removed.

FRENCH ONION SOUP

This soup is comfort in a bowl! It has so much to offer: a rich broth, soft sweet onions, the toasty bread, and of course, ooey-gooey melted cheese!

INGREDIENTS

6 tablespoon butter
2 tablespoon olive oil
3 pounds onions, sliced
2 teaspoons salt
2 teaspoons sugar
6 tablespoons flour
4 quarts beef broth
2 cups red or white wine
1 teaspoon sage
salt and pepper to taste
toasted French bread slices and Gruyère cheese to top soup

DIRECTIONS

Melt butter and oil in large deep skillet. Add the sliced onions. Cook covered over medium-low heat for 20 minutes. Stir occasionally. Remove cover, and add salt and sugar. Continue cooking on high heat, stirring frequently for about 30 minutes or until the onions are browned.

Reduce the heat to low/medium, and stir in the flour. Add one cup of the beef stock and wine, and incorporate into the mix. Add the rest of the liquid, sage, salt, and pepper. Allow the soup to cook/simmer for 1 to 2 hours.

Serve in individual crocks. Place toasted bread and cheese over top the crock. Place in a 300-degree oven and heat until the cheese melts.

ITALIAN EASTER BREAD

Easter bread is made by many Pittsburgh ethnic groups. Some call it paska, and it is a braided loaf that is decorated with colored hard-boiled eggs or rainbow nonpareil candies. It is a sweet bread; my Italian family always added a shot or two of whiskey.

INGREDIENTS

- 1 large cake of yeast
- 1 cup warm water
- 2 tablespoons sugar
- 15 cups flour
- 3 cups sugar
- 15 eggs
- 1/2 cup shortening
- 2 tablespoons whiskey
- 1 teaspoon salt
- 1 teaspoon vanilla
- 1/2 cup butter, melted

DIRECTIONS

Proof the yeast, warm water, and sugar in a small bowl.

In a roaster, mix the flour and salt, and form a well in the center.

In a separate bowl, beat the eggs and sugar until foamy. Add in the melted butter, shortening, vanilla, and whiskey.

Add the proofed yeast mix and the egg mixture to the well in the flour and mix thoroughly. Work and knead the dough for 10–15 minutes. The dough should be smooth and elastic. Place the dough in a very large greased bowl. Cover and set in a warm space, allowing to double in size.

After the bread has doubled in size, punch down, and divide the dough into four equal pieces. Each of the four pieces should be then divided into three long snakes—about 18 inches long.

Braid the three pieces together and place on a greased baking sheet. Cover and allow this to raise until doubled in size. At this point, colored hard-boiled eggs can be added into the braid. Brush each loaf with beaten egg.

Bake at 325 degrees for 30 minutes or until done.

This makes 4 large braided loaves that can be frozen.

ITALIAN ESCAROLE SOUP

Escarole is such a healthy vegetable. Make sure it is washed well. In Pittsburgh, you would say "Wursh" that escarole. We have a dialect that is very unique. We don't clean our house, but rather we "redd up." And those bushes in the backyard with thorns, we call those "jagger" bushes. If you are thirsty in Pittsburgh, you can enjoy a bottle of "pop" but never soda.

INGREDIENTS

1 medium onion, chopped
2 tablespoon olive oil
3–4 cloves garlic, minced
4 cups escarole, washed and chopped
1/2 cup cooked orzo or other small pasta
4 cups chicken stock
Parmesan cheese
salt and pepper

DIRECTIONS

Sauté the onions in olive oil over medium heat until transparent. Add the garlic, and cook lightly. Add chicken stock and escarole. Cook uncovered for 15 minutes. Add the pasta, and cook for an additional 15 minutes. Add salt and pepper to taste.

Serve with Parmesan cheese.

ITALIAN PASTA AND BEANS

My great-aunt Julie DiVittorio lived in the family homestead in Braddock. She often cooked these beans. She had two kitchens! One was in the basement. You could go to the basement the conventional way using the stairs, but if you felt adventurous, you could use that outside stairway that started at ground level. My brother, Tom, and I used to open the two large doors, exposing the stairs. It was dark and damp and always boasted an array of spiders. But at the bottom of the six stairs was the screen door. It was the best scare of the day. It still gives me a shiver just remembering it!

INGREDIENTS

3 tablespoons shortening
1 large onion, chopped
1 large can of diced tomatoes
1 tablespoon fresh Italian parsley
2 teaspoons sugar
2 cans cannelloni beans, undrained
8 ounces ditalini pasta
1 tablespoon Italian cheese
water, if needed

DIRECTIONS

In a medium saucepot, heat shortening, and cook onion until browned. Add the diced tomatoes, sugar, parsley, and salt and pepper. Allow this to cook for 1 to 1 1/2 hours. Add the cannelloni beans with juice, and cook for an additional 20 minutes. If too thick, add water in small amounts to thin.

Cook the ditalini pasta and drain. Add the pasta to the sauce, and bring to a boil. Stir in the Italian cheese, and serve.

JEWISH PASSOVER ROLLS

My parents bought a home in a small community called Eastmont. It was isolated from the rest of the township, which we embraced. Eastmont had its own elementary school, fire department, pool, ball fields, a Lutheran church, a Jewish synagogue, and a Croatian center, where they produced a paper for their members in the United States and in Croatia. Even though there were only four styles of very small houses, we were all certain we were in Brigadoon! Everyone lived and played together, and we were all the same. These delicious rolls came from one of our neighbors.

INGREDIENTS

- 2 cups matzo meal
- 1 teaspoon salt
- 2 tablespoons sugar
- 1 cup water
- 1/2 cup peanut oil
- 4 eggs

DIRECTIONS

Combine the matzo meal, salt, and sugar, and set aside. In a 4-quart heavy saucepan, bring the oil and water to a boil. Add the matzo meal mix to the pot, and mix very well. Remove from the heat.

Beat in the eggs one at a time, making sure the eggs do not scramble. Once all the eggs are mixed in, allow the matzo to rest for 15 minutes.

With oiled hands, form the mix into rolls, and place on a well-greased cookie sheet.

Bake in a 375-degree oven for about 50 minutes or until golden brown.

KIELBASA POTATO CHOWDER

Cathy May is my sister-in-law, who is as close to a sister as I have. She is a very good cook and hard worker. This is her chowder that she makes for her son, Brian. It is perfect on an overcast cold day in Pittsburgh.

INGREDIENTS

1/2 pound smoked kielbasa, cut into 1/2-inch slices
3 strips of bacon, diced
1 small onion
1 clove of garlic, minced
1 1/2 cups chicken broth
1 1/2 cups water
2 medium potatoes, peeled and cubed
1/2 teaspoon chicken bouillon granules
1/4 teaspoon black pepper
1/2 cup chopped fresh spinach or 2 kale leaves
1/2 cup heavy whipping cream or 2 percent milk

DIRECTIONS

In a large skillet, brown the bacon and kielbasa, and drain, leaving 1 teaspoon of the drippings in the pan. Add the onion, and cook over medium heat for 2 or 3 minutes. Add the minced garlic, and cook for an additional minute.

In a saucepan, bring broth and water to a boil. When boiling, add the potatoes, bouillon, and pepper, and allow to cook until the potatoes are tender.

Once the potatoes are tender, add the meat mixture and the spinach or kale. Cook until the greens are wilted. Reduce the heat to a simmer, and add the cream or milk. Cook until the soup is heated through.

This makes 4 cups.

MAMA'S ITALIAN BREAD

This bread is quick and easy. The smell of it baking is heavenly. The Strip District in Pittsburgh isn't a burlesque center. It's the wholesale food capital of the city, where restaurant owners and grandmas shop side by side for everything from just baked biscotti to kangaroo meat. It is a plethora of tastes, smells, and sights—all having to do with food. And much of the food has ethnic roots. So on Saturdays and before holidays (especially Thanksgiving and Christmas), Pittsburghers flock to the Strip to buy the needs for their family's holiday feasts. The smell of this bread with the herbs roasting on top reminds me of the wonderful Strip District of Pittsburgh.

INGREDIENTS

3 cups warm water (110 degrees)
2 teaspoons white sugar
7 cups flour
1 tablespoon active dry yeast
1 teaspoon salt
assorted herbs for top of bread

DIRECTIONS

Place warm water in metal or ceramic bowl, and allow the sugar to dissolve and proof the yeast. Stir in 4 cups of flour, and beat until smooth. Cover this, and allow to rest for 15 minutes.

Combine the remaining flour and salt, and mix into the bread to form a stiff dough. Knead the bread until smooth and soft. Turn dough into a greased bowl, and cover. Allow to double in size.

Once it has doubled, punch down, and form into three loaves. Grease three heavy cookie sheets, and sprinkle with corn meal. Place a loaf on each cookie sheet, cover, and allow to rise again.

Once the loaves have risen, mist with water, and sprinkle with seasonings of your choice. Mist occasionally, and rotate the cookie sheet once while baking.

Bake in a 450-degree oven until golden brown.

McCALL'S IRISH SODA BREAD

My dad's family (Lutton and McCall) came from Ireland, England, and Scotland. They settled in the US around 1750. This was a favorite bread of theirs. They were all big bowlers. Generally, Pittsburgh has a bowling alley in just about every town. The Luttons bowled weekly; my dad bowled duck pins. I inherited the trait… I can't say the same for Les.

We were in a wonderful couple's league for a year until one night. We met in the back of the lanes.

I asked, "How did you do, dear?"

He said, "Well, I bowled a 98. How did you do?"

"Well, I bowled a 243."

And with that, we were done bowling.

INGREDIENTS

4 cups all-purpose flour plus 1/2 cup
1 teaspoon baking soda
1 1/2 teaspoon salt
6 tablespoons sugar
6 tablespoons cold butter cut into small cubes
1 3/4 cup buttermilk
2 large eggs lightly beaten
1 1/2 teaspoons vanilla
1 cup currants or raisins dusted in flour

DIRECTIONS

Preheat oven to 375 degrees.

In a mixer, combine the 4 cups of flour, baking soda, salt, and sugar. Once the dry ingredients are blended, add the chopped butter, and mix on low until the butter is incorporated in the mixture. When the flour is completely mixed, change the mixer to the dough hook.

In a separate bowl, mix the beaten eggs with the buttermilk and vanilla, and add to the flour mix slowly. Add the dusted currants. Add the 1/2 cup of flour, 1 tablespoon at a time, until the bread pulls from the sides of the bowl and forms a doughball.

continued

Turn on to a floured surface, and knead a few times to form a large round loaf. Cut an X in the top. Place on greased sheet, and bake 45 to 50 minutes until cake tester comes out clean.
Bread can be drizzled with a simple icing.

PASTA E FAGIOLI

My great-grandmother Mariantonetta DeFalco Capezzuto was the grand matriarch of our family. Her beauty was stunning, and she was so loved and respected. My mom often said that Grandma had such a wide knowledge that she knew what to do no matter what happened. My favorite memory is when she called my brother Little Porkie in Italian. Oh, did I laugh, and oh, was he not happy! I am thrilled to have her portrait on display in my living room.

The following is the exact verbatim recipe from my great-grandmother's cooking notes from Italy. I understand it lacks some specific measurements of ingredients, but in the end, it all comes together. Sometimes cooking doesn't have to be an exact science, just a work of love.

INGREDIENTS

oil – small amount–2 tablespoons
1 large onion, chopped
28 ounce can of tomatoes, processed in a blender
1 teaspoon sugar or more to your taste
salt and pepper to taste
handful of fresh parsley
½ can water using the 28 ounce can
large glass (12 ounce) water
2–15 ounce cans cannellini beans, undrained
2 cans of water using a 15 ounce cannellini bean can
6 ounce spaghetti, boiled and drained
Several slices of Italian bread, torn into pieces
Drizzle of olive oil

DIRECTIONS

In a large heavy pot, put a little oil. Chop a large onion, and add to the pot and brown slowly. While the onions brown, push a large can of tomatoes through a sieve to puree. Put the tomatoes in a smaller pot, and add 1 teaspoon of sugar, salt, pepper, and lots of Italian flat-leaf parsley.

continued

Bring to a boil. Add 1/2 can of water. Reduce and cook slowly.

Pour the cooked tomatoes into the onion, and cook slowly 1 1/2 hours, adding water from a large glass of water a little at a time.

Add 2 cans of cannellini beans and their juice and 2 cans of water. Allow this to cook for 20 to 30 minutes

In separate pot, boil 6 ounces of spaghetti and add. Serve warm.

(Panada is a type of bread soup.) On the second day, take remaining pasta e fagioli, and add pieces of Italian bread with a little oil. Gently fold in, and heat and serve.

PEPPERONI BREAD

Pittsburgh is home to hundreds of ethnic clubs. We have attended many functions and dinners at our local Italian Club. The clubs represent Italians, Germans, Polish, Ukrainians, Hungarians, Irish, Croatians, African American, Serbians, and other ethnicities. The German Teutonia Mannerchoir Club in the North Side neighborhood, called Deutschtown, has nearly 2,500 members. Numerous Polish clubs scattered throughout Western Pennsylvania have over 600 members. Many ethnic clubs are open daily for food and drink, while others maintain weekend hours, in addition to their membership meetings and functions.

INGREDIENTS

3/4 cup sliced pepperoni
1/2 cup grated Romano cheese
1 cup shredded mozzarella cheese
2 tablespoon chopped parsley
1 loaf frozen bread

DIRECTIONS

Roll thawed bread dough in to a large rectangle. Mix all the ingredients together, and spread on the dough. Roll up the rectangle of dough like a jelly roll, and pinch the seam to seal it. Place seam side down on a lightly greased baking sheet. Brush crust with melted butter, and sprinkle with Italian seasoning.

Bake at 375 degrees for 40 minutes or until golden brown and done.

PITTSBURGH'S FAMOUS NUT BREAD

In the sixties and seventies, Pittsburghers loved their nut and fruit breads. I remember always seeing an array of breads at holidays as well as wedding and bridal showers. At that time, I remember my mom having a bread that she had to add to and divide and then find a friend that would take it off her hands. It was actually a worry—stressful even! Add, mix, and bake every so many days, or else! It reminded me of the blob growing on our kitchen counter!

INGREDIENTS

2 1/2 cups flour
4 teaspoons baking powder
1 teaspoon salt
2 tablespoons unsalted butter
2/3 cup sugar
2 eggs
1 1/2 cup pecans or walnuts, toasted and chopped
1 cup whole milk

DIRECTIONS

Sift together the flour, baking powder, and salt, and set aside. Cream together the butter and sugar. Add the eggs to the butter-and-sugar mixture one at a time, and beat until light and fluffy. Add the nuts, and continue to beat. Alternatively, add in the sifted flour mix and the milk, and beat until well blended. Pour into a greased and floured 9-by-5-inch loaf pan.

Bake at 350 degrees for 1 hour or until tested done.

Cool completely, and remove from pan. Keep wrapped in plastic or foil wrap, and store in the refrigerator.

PIZZA DOUGH

Pittsburgh has the fifth-largest Italian population in the United States. It's amazing to think that in 1930 one out of every six Pittsburgh residents was an immigrant.

INGREDIENTS

4 cups flour
1 egg
1 tablespoon salt
2 tablespoons sugar
2 tablespoons shortening, softened
1 package yeast proofed in 1/4 cup warm water and 1 cup warm milk

DIRECTIONS

Dissolve yeast in warm milk and water.

Place the dry ingredients in a large bowl, and mix with the soft shortening by hand until the shortening is completely incorporated into the flour mix.

Add the egg and yeast mixture together, and form a dough. Knead the dough until it is smooth. Form dough into a ball, and place in a lightly oiled bowl. Cover, and let dough rise one hour. Punch down, and form to pan. Add sauce and toppings and cheese.

Drizzle with olive oil, and bake—usually at 425 degrees for 10–15 minutes or until cheese is golden and crust is brown.

SAUSAGE, PASTA, AND BEANS

Our family home had this attic. To my brother, Tom, and me, it was an adventure that we never passed up! First of all, to get to the stairs to the attic, you had to go through a secret passage in my cousin Anthony's closet! At the top of the stairs, there was a large room filled with treasures and a sizable steamer trunk with the destination labels from all those who used it to travel here from Italy! I am honored to have that special trunk now as the coffee table in my great room!

INGREDIENTS

1 pound of loose Italian hot sausage, cooked and drained
3 tablespoons oil
1 can of cannellini beans, undrained
1 large onion, chopped
1/2 pound ditali pasta cooked, drained
1 large 28-ounce can crushed tomatoes
1 tablespoon Parmesan cheese
2 tablespoon parsley
1 stalk of celery, thinly chopped
salt and pepper to taste

DIRECTIONS

In a skillet, brown and drain the sausage, and set aside.

In a large heavy saucepot, heat oil, and sauté the chopped onion until it starts to brown. Add the can of tomatoes, parsley, and salt and pepper, and allow to cook for 1 to 1 1/2 hours on medium to low heat. Add the cannellini beans with the juice, and allow to cook and additional 20 minutes. Add the chopped celery and browned sausage.

Cook the ditali pasta, and drain. Add the pasta to the tomato, sausage, and bean mix, and let come to a boil. Add the Parmesan cheese, and stir well.

Serve with Italian bread.

TORTILLA SOUP

I have made this soup in large amounts for Les to take to school when the teachers had in-service days. It's a favorite! Our dear friends Tom and Diana Clouser once traded me a tabletop fryer for a pot of this soup!

INGREDIENTS

3 14.5-ounce cans chicken broth
3 large cans crushed tomatoes
2 cups water
1 medium-sized jar medium or mild salsa
1 bay leaf
2 cloves garlic, minced
2 teaspoons cumin
cayenne pepper to taste
1 tablespoon chili powder
1 tablespoon granulated sugar or to taste
2 tablespoons olive oil
4 chicken breast, grilled
1 large onion, chopped
2 cans black beans, drained
2 cans chopped tomatoes
3 cans Mexican-style corn
cilantro or flat-leaf parsley

DIRECTIONS

In a large soup pot, sauté chopped onion and minced garlic until transparent. Add chicken broth, crushed tomatoes, and water, and allow to cook for 10 minutes. Add bay leaf and seasonings. Seasonings can be changed for specific taste needs. Allow this to cook and come to a boil. Reduce the heat to simmer, and add the beans, the parsley or cilantro, and the grilled chicken, which should be cut into strips. Allow soup to simmer for a couple of hours.

Serve with fried tortilla strips or broken tortilla chips, chopped green onions, shredded cheddar or Mexican cheese, and/or a dollop of sour cream.

ZUCCHINI-AND-PEPPERONI BREAD BAKE

I find this a quirky recipe. I would not normally put these two items together, but it works. Aunt Julie (ZiaZia) made this often.

Pittsburgh is a quirky town. We have museums dedicated to bicycles, genetically altered things, colors, Knick Knacks (Knick Knacks are big in Pittsburgh), an old jail, unusual musical instruments, model railroads, antique photography, and religious relics. Pittsburgh actually has the most religious relics of any city, just short of the Vatican! Put that in your pope, and smoke it!

INGREDIENTS

3 cups zucchini, grated
1 cup pepperoni, diced
1 cup flour-based baking mix
4 eggs, beaten
1 cup shredded mozzarella
1/2 cup olive oil
1/2 cup Parmesan cheese
1 tablespoon Italian parsley
1 medium onion, grated
pinch basil
salt and pepper to taste

DIRECTIONS

Beat together the oil and eggs. Add the baking mix, and mix well.
Add all the other ingredients, and place in a greased 9-inch-by-13-inch dish.
Bake in a 350-degree oven for 25–30 minutes until golden brown, and set.
Cut into squares, and serve warm.

PITTSBURGH HOUSES

Pittsburgh is a city of neighborhoods. Back at the height of the steel industry, many houses were built near mills, mines, and factories. Most workers were able to walk to work. The building codes were not as today's. Many houses were two feet or less from the next. Most had just a narrow walkway between buildings, and some not even that.

Still to this day, when we see a house that is a foot or less from the next, questions pop into our mind. Which house was built first? What happens if the sides of the house need repaired? How do workers get in there to fix it? It seems that it is impossible for anyone to get between the houses to work!

Some housing plans for coal mines consisted of identical homes, one after the other. The millhouses were always two stories, sometimes with an attic. Most of those houses had one bathroom, usually on the second floor. That raised the problem for many of our aging parents who lived in those homes of having to climb a long set of stairs to the second floor every time that they needed to use the bathroom. Obviously, that was not a good situation. Also having a large family in one house with only one toilet is a conundrum.

That is why many families opted to install the infamous "Pittsburgh toilet" in their basement. This is a toilet in the basement with no walls around it and is often on a raised concrete pad to provide for the plumbing. Sometimes it was surrounded by a shower curtain—but was sometimes not. However, when there was a need and nowhere else to go, the Pittsburgh toilet in the middle of the basement looked pretty good!

I have a dear friend, LaVerne Lokay. She is ninety years old and was raised in a two-story house with her sisters. With only two bedrooms in the house, LaVerne and her older sister slept in the attic. The attic had no heat, and with the harsh Pittsburgh winters, it would get very cold. LaVerne's mother collected old heavy winter coats and sewed a quilt for each girl—a remarkable, caring effort to keep her girls warm! People back then had to work with the resources they had at hand. LaVerne's mother was truly ingenious. In the summer, LaVerne and her sister had to endure the excessive heat since the attic had such little ventilation. Making do with what they had, Laverne's mother and father allowed the two girls to sleep on the front porch on those very hot nights.

It seems like a world away—those times when people of Pittsburgh made the best of the things they had. I sometimes think we were better off during that time than now. Sometimes simple is better.

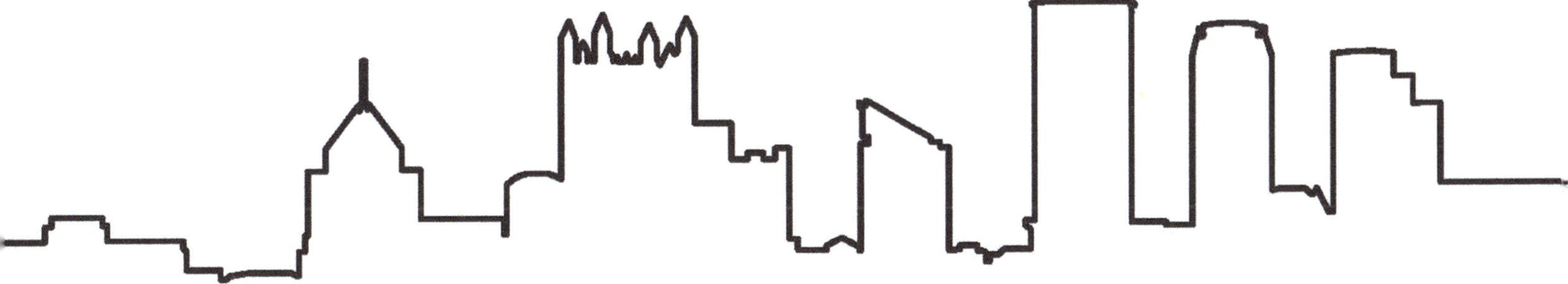

SALADS AND SIDE DISHES

AUSTRIAN POTATO PIE

My wonderful mother-in-law, Hilda Niehl, was from Austria-Hungary. I made this for her, and she so enjoyed it. She told me it reminded her of the food her mother, Julia Sholder, made for her and her ten brothers and sisters on Three Hill in Wilkins Township, Pittsburgh. (The hills were often named for the coal mines that dotted the Western Pennsylvania landscape.)

INGREDIENTS

pie crusts, top and bottom (homemade or store-bought)
potatoes, enough to layer the dish twice, sliced and seasoned
1/2 pound bacon, cooked and chopped
3 eggs, hard-boiled eggs, sliced
1/3 pound Swiss cheese, sliced
salt and pepper to taste

DIRECTIONS

Place the pie or pastry crust in bottom of a ceramic dish.

Layer the sliced seasoned raw potatoes. Next, place a layer of the cooked bacon and the sliced hard-boiled eggs. Layer the sliced Swiss cheese, and finish with a final layer of sliced potatoes that have been seasoned.

Place the pie or pastry crust on top, and seal it like a fruit pie.

Bake using the following temperature-and-time settings:

- 400 degrees for 20 minutes
- 350 degrees for 1 hour
- 300 degrees for 10 minutes

Serve this at room temperature to slightly warm.

AN ITALIAN GIRL'S SPAETZLE

This spaetzle is perfect for the Polish haluski or even mac 'n' cheese. There is nothing quite as homey as buttered spaetzle. There are quite a few German restaurants in Pittsburgh, and each offers their take on spaetzle. I have not been disappointed yet!

INGREDIENTS

1 1/2 cups flour
4 eggs
1/3 cup sour cream
1/4–1/3 cup milk
1 teaspoon salt
1/2 teaspoon pepper
1/4 cup butter

DIRECTIONS

Mix the flour and eggs together. Add the sour cream, and mix with a wooden spoon until thick.

Add the milk to cut the batter until it resembles thick pancake batter.

Using a spaetzle maker or by pressing through a colander or sieve, drop batter into a pot of salted boiling water.

Stirring constantly, bring water back to a boil. Then reduce heat, and simmer for 10 minutes.

Drain and toss with butter.

Add salt and pepper to taste.

BAKED CAULIFLOWER AND EGGS

Cauliflower is a great vegetable. It grows very well in Western Pennsylvania because of our warm summer days and cool nights. Give this a chance. The white sauce brings the flavors together quite nicely. Test to make sure the cauliflower is cooked before serving.

INGREDIENTS

Main ingredients:

- 1 head of cauliflower cut into medium flowerets
- 4 hard-boiled eggs
- white sauce
- salt and pepper to taste
- bread crumbs

For the white sauce:

- 1/2 cup butter
- 1/2 cup flour
- 2 cups milk
- salt to taste

DIRECTIONS

Cut cauliflower into medium-sized flowerets.

Slice the hard-boiled eggs.

Layer the cauliflower and eggs in an 8-by-4-inch buttered casserole.

To prepare the white sauce, melt butter in pan and stir in flour. Season with salt, and allow to bubble and cook for 3 minutes. Do not allow to burn. Add milk, and whisk to a smooth sauce.

Pour white sauce over the layered cauliflower and eggs. Top with bread crumbs (you can dot with butter if you wish).

Bake in a 350-degree oven for 30 minutes or until the cauliflower is tender.

BAKED ITALIAN EGGPLANT

This is Pittsburgh Italian. It is offered in many restaurants and even made into sandwiches and hoagies. Being Italian, we ate eggplant regularly hot from the oven and even many cold eggplant sandwiches with the leftovers! Such a treat!

INGREDIENTS

1–2 eggplants, peeled and sliced into 1/2-inch slices and soaked in salted water for 1 hour
flour, seasoned with garlic and salt
4 beaten eggs
spaghetti sauce
Parmesan cheese

DIRECTIONS

After the eggplant has been soaked, press several slices at a time between your palms to remove the excess water. Dip each slice into the seasoned flour and then into the beaten egg. Fry immediately in 1/2 inch of heated oil. Allow the eggplant to drain.

Place spaghetti sauce in the bottom of a 9-by-13-inch baking dish, and layer the eggplant, covering each layer with sauce and cheese.

Bake at 325 degrees until completely heated throughout.

BREAD-AND-BUTTER PICKLES

Pittsburgh is known for its celebration of everything pickled. Each year, the Roberto Clemente Bridge is closed and becomes Picklesburgh! It has received national attention and is sponsored by many large companies. It is quite the *big dill*! These are wonderful pickles, and they stay crunchy because of the ice.

INGREDIENTS

6 medium to large cucumbers
2 onions
2 tablespoons mustard seed
1 small bag ice
2 tablespoons pickling spice
3 cups cider vinegar
5 cups sugar
1/2 cup salt

DIRECTIONS

Cut the cucumbers into slices and the onions into pieces.

In a large bowl, layer the cucumbers and onions with a layer of ice and then salt. Repeat until all the cucumbers and onions are covered.

Let stand for 3 hours. Drain and rinse well.

Cook and bring to a boil the cider vinegar, sugar, and spices. Once the mixture has reached a boil, add the cucumbers and onions, and cook until it reaches a boil once again.

During this time, prepare your jars and lids. In a warm pint jar, spoon some of the liquid in the bottom and pack your cucumbers and onions. Fill the jar with liquid until it is 1/4 inch from the top.

Place warmed lids on each, and close each jar—but not tightly. Place in a water bath, and process for 10 minutes in a rolling boil.

Once the jars are removed, make sure the jar has sealed and they can be tightly closed.

CHICKPEA-AND-PASTA SALAD

This recipe is from my cousin Marie DiVittorio Cifone. Being Italian, there were so many Maries in the family that usually we call her Dolly. When she was young, she was a wonderful ballet dancer. Honestly, our planet is blessed to have her. She is so kind and thoughtful. Such a good person!

INGREDIENTS

For the salad:

- 2 cups pasta (shells or springs)
- fresh broccoli florets
- 2 medium tomatoes, chopped
- 1 can chickpeas, drained

For the dressing:

- 1/2 cup oil
- 1/3 cup cider vinegar or rice wine vinegar
- salt, pepper, garlic powder, and oregano to taste

DIRECTIONS

Cook pasta and drain. Rinse lightly with cold water.
Combine all the ingredients together.
Prepare the dressing, and pour over the pasta and toss.
Cover and chill for several hours.
Serve chilled.

BROCCOLI IN LEMON

Who knew that broccoli originated in Italy! A member of the cabbage family, it has a wide variety of uses. This is a refreshing salad that is so simple and offers such a unique taste experience.

INGREDIENTS

4 heads of broccoli, trimmed into stalks
3 ripe lemons or more to taste
6 garlic cloves, chopped into large pieces
1/4 cup olive oil or more to taste

DIRECTIONS

Parcook the broccoli in hot water. Boil just until tender.
Rinse under cold water to stop the cooking, and drain.
Place broccoli in a bowl. Squeeze the lemons over the broccoli, and add the garlic.
Pour the olive oil over everything and toss.
Refrigerate overnight, and serve cold.

FRIED GREEN TOMATOES

There is nothing better than a fried green tomato. We have been enjoying them for years. I have struggled with the seasoning mix to dip them in before frying. This is our favorite. My kids—Jake, Adam, and Juli—eat these before they make it to the dinner table!

INGREDIENTS

4 green tomatoes, washed and sliced
2 cups flour
2 teaspoons salt
2 teaspoons granular garlic
1 teaspoon black pepper
3 eggs, beaten with 1 tablespoon of water
oil for frying

DIRECTIONS

Wash and dry the green tomatoes. Slice the tomatoes more thin than thick.

Combine the flour, salt, and pepper, and place in a bowl.

Place the beaten egg mix in another bowl.

Put about 1/2 inch of oil in a heavy frying pan. Dip each slice into the egg mix and then the flour mixture, and fry until golden brown.

Drain on paper towels, and serve warm.

GINGERED PEARS

I have been told that pears ripen best off the tree! Sometimes the pears you buy in the store are mature but not quite ripe. They need some time to come to their best taste. The more time you give them to ripen and soften, the better your pear will be!

INGREDIENTS

2 pounds fresh pears, peeled and sliced
2 cups water
2 cups sugar
1 cinnamon stick
peel of 1/2 lemon
1 teaspoon whole cloves
2 tablespoons freshly grated ginger

DIRECTIONS

Peel and slice pears and set aside.

In a heavy saucepot, combine all the ingredients except the pears. Mix together, and place on medium heat. Bring this to boil, and add the pears. Reduce heat to a simmer, and allow the pears to poach in the syrup until tender and transparent. Once cooked, remove the pot from the heat, and allow the pears to cool in the syrup.

Serve with pork or chicken.

GELATIN LAYERED SALAD

If you have a day to hang out, this is a great dessert/salad to put together. It takes time to choose your color scheme, make the white layer, and keep it warm, then make the colored layers. Put the dish in the refrigerator, keeping it level, and begin the day of layering. In the end, wherever you take this, you will be the praise of everyone and immediately forget and forgive yourself for feeling so angry that you have spent so much time on a single dessert made of colored gelatin. Choose flavors/colors to compliment your theme (e.g., cherry/red and blueberry/blue for patriotic holiday/theme).

INGREDIENTS

- 4 3-ounce packages of flavored gelatin
- 1 1/2 cup water (for each package of flavored gelatin)
- 2 packages unflavored gelatin
- 2 cups whole milk
- 1 cup sugar
- 1/2 cup cold water
- 2 cups sour cream
- 2 1/2 teaspoons clear vanilla

DIRECTIONS

In a heavy saucepan, bring the milk to a boil, and add the sugar. Reduce the heat to medium, and whisk until all the sugar is completely dissolved. Set the pan aside on a back burner of the stove.

In a small dish, dissolve the unflavored gelatin in 1/2 cup cold water, and whisk into the milk and sugar mix. Finally, add the sour cream and vanilla, and beat until smooth. Allow to sit in the saucepan throughout the duration of the process. If the mix should start to set, turn the heat to a minimum setting, and mix for a short time just to return the mix to the creamy consistency.

To layer the gelatin, begin with one flavor of gelatin, mixing it with 1 cup hot water. Once it has dissolved, add the 1/2 cup cold water. Pour into a 13-by-9-inch dish.

Allow the gelatin to set before adding the 1 1/2 cup of the creamy white layer. Once the white layer is set, repeat the process until you have a beautiful layered dish that will be the highlight of your event.

Note: Various dishes and molds can be used, but the amounts of each layer will vary by the size of the dish or mold.

HOMEMADE CROUTONS

So buttery… Such a great crunch to any salad or soup!

INGREDIENTS

8 slices of day-old fresh bread, cut into 1/2-inch cubes
8 tablespoons salted butter
2 tablespoons Parmesan cheese, grated
1 tablespoon dried parsley
1 teaspoon oregano
1 teaspoon garlic powder
1/2 teaspoon onion powder

DIRECTIONS

Melt butter in a skillet, and add the seasonings. In a large bowl, place the cubed bread, sprinkle with the Parmesan cheese, and pour melted butter over the cubes. Toss and spread on a cookie sheet.

Bake in a 325-degree oven for 20 minutes or until golden. Stir often.

ITALIAN ESCAROLE

Escarole is a funny thing. I remember my mother, Angie, struggling to get all the escarole layered in her pot. It was heaping and was like herding cats! She would tuck leaves here and there and hope that once she put that lid on, it was all in there. The ironic thing was, by the end of the cooking, there was barely anything there. It really cooks down. I remember saying, "Ma! Where's it all gone?" She would mutter in Italian words I wasn't allowed to use!

INGREDIENTS

1 large escarole, washed and cut into three sections
1 can of small or medium black olives, drained
1–2 cans of anchovies, drained
2 tablespoons capers, drained
2 cloves of garlic, crushed
salt and pepper
olive oil

DIRECTIONS

After the escarole has been washed, layer the escarole in the pot with the salt, pepper, anchovies, capers, and garlic. Sprinkle with olive oil.

Cover tightly.

Allow to cook very slowly for 2 1/2 hours.

ITALIAN BREAD-STUFFED FINGER PEPPERS

These peppers are soooo Italian. Please don't let those anchovies and capers scare you. They actually melt into the flavor of the stuffing. Be patient cooking these. They need to cook through, and a gradual low/ medium heat is best. My mom, Angie, used a large cast-iron skillet, and she would go about her work in the kitchen as they cooked.

INGREDIENTS

8–10 green sweet or hot finger peppers, tops removed
3/4 loaf of stale Italian bread or 1 can of Italian bread crumbs
1 tin of anchovies with capers, chopped
1 can black olives, sliced in half
1 clove garlic finely chopped
2 tablespoons olive oil
sprinkle of water
salt, pepper, oregano and parsley to taste, finely chopped

DIRECTIONS

Grate the Italian bread, or place the bread crumbs into a mixing bowl. Add seasonings and chopped garlic. Work in the chopped anchovies and capers. Add the olive oil and a sprinkle of water. Work this mixture well, and add the black olives. The stuffing should look wet.

Carefully stuff each pepper so peppers do not tear.

In a large skillet with oil, slowly fry the stuffed peppers over medium to low heat. Carefully turn each pepper as it browns. Once all the peppers are browned, cover the skillet with a lid, and allow to cook through.

Serve warm or at room temperature.

ITALIAN ROASTED RED PEPPERS

I know you can buy these peppers in a jar, but if you can make them, they are really worth the time and effort. My mom, Angie, would make platters of these, and the visual of those vibrant red strips of peppers dotted with white pieces of garlic and the deep green leaves of parsley was beyond stunning. They are wonderful on a sandwich or in a salad or even by themselves.

INGREDIENTS

fresh red peppers, unwashed
salt
minced fresh garlic
olive oil
fresh Italian parsley or fresh basil

DIRECTIONS

Place each pepper on a gas grill set on high or directly on the burner of a gas stove set on high. Allow pepper to blacken completely. If using an electric stove, place in the oven set at a high temperature (400 degrees), and allow pepper to blacken.

When complete, work off the blackened area but *do not* use water. Cut the peppers into strips, and lay them on a large serving dish. Sprinkle with olive oil, a small amount of salt, minced garlic, and the parsley or basil.

Cover tightly with plastic wrap, and refrigerate overnight.

Serve cold.

ITALIAN SPINACH AND EGGS

My mom loved making this dish. We always enjoyed it. I don't think my brother, Tom, or I ever realized that we were eating spinach. When she put it in an egg bake, it tasted great. She was so clever! She always thought of helpful things like making sure we put a plastic bread bag on our feet before we put our snow boots on. After hours of sled riding, our feet were always dry. Good job, Mom!

INGREDIENTS

10 ounces of spinach
4 tablespoons olive oil
2 cloves of garlic, minced
1 cup water
3 large eggs
1/2 cup Italian cheese
salt and pepper to taste

DIRECTIONS

In a skillet, heat oil and lightly cook garlic.

Add the spinach and 1 cup of water, and allow the spinach to cook thoroughly. Season with salt and pepper. Continue until the spinach is cooked.

Beat the eggs and add the Italian cheese. Then pour the mixture into the skillet with the spinach.

Cook slowly until the eggs are finished.

Serve warm.

ITALIAN ZUCCHINI (OR PEPPERS) AND EGGS

Gagoots! This is known to many Pittsburgh Italians as gagoots. It is a lovely dish when you are able to flip it in one piece. It is very tasty. For those trying to follow a low-carb diet, you can't beat eggs and sautéed peppers or zucchini. It's a nice side dish with most meats!

INGREDIENTS

2–3 medium zucchini, washed and sliced (or green peppers, seeded and sliced)
1/2 cup olive oil or enough oil to sauté the vegetables in
4 eggs, beaten
1/2 teaspoon garlic powder
salt and pepper to taste

DIRECTIONS

Sauté zucchini or peppers in a large skillet until zucchini is softened or the peppers are browned. Add the beaten eggs, and allow the eggs to surround the vegetables. Cook over medium/low heat.

When you can see that the mix is firming and almost cooked on the underside, take a large plate, and flip and return to the pan to cook on the other side to finish the dish.

If this is too difficult, you can cover the pan so that the eggs will cook on the top as well. You may have to pop some of the bubbles that form as it cooks through.

Serve warm in wedges.

JULI'S GARLIC MASHED RED POTATOES

This is the first recipe that my daughter, Julia Rose, created. We really love them. They have become our Thanksgiving potatoes. (We save the gravy for the stuffing and turkey!)

INGREDIENTS

15–20 medium red potatoes, washed with skins on
3 cloves garlic, crushed
1 cup butter
1/2 teaspoon seasoned salt
3/4 cup half and half
1/4 cup white sugar
1/2 teaspoon garlic powder

DIRECTIONS

Boil the potatoes and one clove of crushed garlic in salted water. Cook the potatoes until they are soft and an inserted knife slides easily through each potato. Drain and return the potatoes to the pot.

Add the butter and mash the potatoes and butter together until the butter is completely melted.

In a small bowl, mix together the half and half, sugar, seasoned salt, the remaining crushed garlic, and garlic powder.

Pour into the mashed potatoes, and beat until smooth and creamy.

Serve warm.

MANDARIN-ORANGE-AND-ONION SALAD

The colors alone of this salad are wonderful! I like to see a variety of colors and textures on a brunch table, so I love to add this quick and easy salad.

INGREDIENTS

2 cans mandarin oranges, drained
1 large Bermuda onion, sliced
1 avocado, sliced
1/3 cup olive oil
5 tablespoons orange juice
4 tablespoons rice wine vinegar
1/2 teaspoon salt
1/2 teaspoon freshly ground pepper
1 cup pecans, toasted (optional)
romaine lettuce

DIRECTIONS

Slice onion and avocado, and separate oranges. Carefully, mix them together.

Combine the orange juice, rice wine vinegar, olive oil, and seasonings, and pour over the oranges, avocado, and onions.

Toss together.

Chill for 2 hours before serving on romaine leaves.

LES' POTATO PANCAKES

We have always considered ourselves to be German, even though my mother's family allegedly came from Austria-Hungary. My dad's ancestors were said to come from somewhere around Cologne, Germany. So when I was a kid, it seemed natural that Mom would make a German favorite—potato pancakes. She would put a layer of hot oil in her cast-iron skillet and drop the batter in. The pancakes looked like brown snowflakes with a crisp lattice around the edges. The recipe below makes the production a lot healthier by cutting down on the oil, but they still taste like I remember them from a long time ago. Sometimes they get eaten right off the griddle, never making it to the table! (*written by Les Niehl*)

INGREDIENTS

5 pounds white russet potatoes
2 eggs
1–2 medium onion(s)
2–3 tablespoons flour
vegetable oil

DIRECTIONS

Peel and cut the potatoes and onions into 1 inch to 2 inch pieces.

Using the blades on a food processor, drop the potatoes and onions into the processor, making a slurry. Empty the processor into a large mixing bowl.

Repeat the procedure, but occasionally, add an egg and some flour to the potatoes and onions in the processor.

After all the potatoes and onions have been processed along with the eggs and flour, stir the mixing bowl until you have a thin batter. If you prefer thicker pancakes, add more flour. For thinner pancakes, add less flour.

Brush a griddle or large skillet with vegetable oil, and put it on medium high to high.

Ladle enough batter onto the griddle to make 3-inch diameter pancakes. Continue to brush oil on the surface of the griddle or skillet intermittently so that the pancakes fry to a golden brown. When finished, put the pancakes onto a plate covered with paper towels to drain.

Pancakes can be served with salt and pepper, cottage cheese, sour cream, shredded cheddar cheese, or applesauce.

Sehr gut! (Very good!)

MY FAVORITE NIECE'S MILLION BEAN BAKE (KATHY SHEPHERD)

Kathy…such a warm, gracious person, so welcoming and positive with amazing strength, faith, and grace.

INGREDIENTS

2 28-ounce cans pork 'n beans, undrained
1 15-ounce can kidney beans, undrained
1 15-ounce can green beans, drained
1 15-ounce can yellow beans, drained
1 15-ounce can chickpeas
1 15-ounce can black beans, drained
1 15-ounce can butter beans, drained
1 small can tomato paste
1 can tomato soup
1 cup brown sugar
1/2 cup onion, chopped
1/2 cup red pepper, chopped
1 1/2 pound sweet sausage
1/2 pound hot sausage

DIRECTIONS

Combine all the beans and chickpeas in a large casserole dish, and set aside.

In a bowl, combine the tomato paste, tomato soup, brown sugar, chopped onion, and red pepper.

If sausage is in the casings, remove and brown in a skillet. Break up the sausage meat, and drain when cooked.

Mix the sausage and beans together. Pour the sauce over the mix and stir.

Cover the dish with foil, and bake for 45 minutes in a 350-degree oven.

This dish can be made ahead and frozen.

ORIENTAL NOODLES

I could eat these noodles every day. My mom loved Asian food. The local Asian restaurant brought her many a dinner. Her last birthday in her home, she actually ordered an entire duck—and ate it all herself! The girl could eat!

INGREDIENTS

3 cloves garlic, smashed
1/3 cup oil
1/3 cup soy sauce
1/3 cup rice wine vinegar
1/4 cup brown sugar
3 tablespoons honey
2 tablespoons sesame seeds, toasted
1 1/2 teaspoons red pepper flakes
1 pound noodles (lo mein or linguini), cooked and drained

DIRECTIONS

Cook noodles, drain, and set aside.

In a skillet, toast the sesame seeds, and set aside.

In a heavy saucepot, combine all ingredients except sesame seeds and red pepper flakes. Bring to a boil. Allow to boil for one minute. Remove from heat, and add the toasted sesame seeds and red pepper flakes.

These noodles pair very well with matchstick-cut carrots, zucchini, squash, and chicken or shrimp.

Sauté items until fully cooked, and toss with sauce and noodles.

Serve.

POLENTA

Polenta can be a confusing thing. It looks like grits, but it's not! Truth is, polenta is made from ground yellow corn. Grits, on the other hand, are made from ground white corn. Polenta originates in central Italy. It is coarser than its cousin, grits. Each product is prepared and presented very differently. Polenta is a dish made most often in many Pittsburgh homes. Grits are usually offered at large national restaurant chains.

INGREDIENTS

2 cups of polenta
6 cups of water, salted
8 tablespoons butter
4 ounces mozzarella cheese
1 pound of sliced mushrooms
2 green peppers, sliced
1 medium onion, chopped
1/3 pound of bulk Italian hot sausage, crumbled
1 cup Italian spaghetti sauce
Parmesan cheese
3 tablespoons butter

DIRECTIONS

Add the polenta slowly to 6 cups salted boiling water, stirring constantly. Cook for 20 minutes.

Add the 8 tablespoons of butter and mozzarella cheese. Add salt and pepper to taste.

Pour onto a greased cookie sheet. Bake at 350 degrees for 20–30 minutes or until a knife inserted comes out clean. Cut into 3-by-4-inch rounds.

Sauté the sausage, drain, and set aside.

Sauté onion, mushrooms, and green peppers. Combine them with cooked sausage and tomato sauce.

In a 13-by-9-inch dish, and layer the polenta and mushroom-sausage-pepper-onion-tomato sauce mix.

Top with Parmesan cheese, and dot with butter.

Bake in a 350-degree oven for 15–20 minutes.

SAUERKRAUT

Making sauerkraut is not difficult. We try to make a batch to use for our New Year's celebration. When we don't have fresh sauerkraut, this is my recipe for store-bought. We cook it slow and long so it browns and develops great flavor. It is the perfect compliment to a pork roast.

INGREDIENTS

3 32-ounce jars sauerkraut, rinsed and drained
1 small to medium onion, thinly sliced
1 small apple, grated
4 tablespoons dark brown sugar
1 tablespoon caraway seeds
2 cups water or apple juice

DIRECTIONS

Mix all ingredients together.

Place in ovenproof pan or dish, and allow to bake in a medium oven (325 degrees) for 2 hours or more. Cook with a foil or lid covering.

This can be cooked on top of the stove using a heavy pot over low to medium heat. Always cover the pot and stir periodically to make sure the kraut doesn't dry out.

STRAWBERRY-AND-ORANGE FOOLS

These oranges are a nice touch for a brunch or breakfast. The colors catch every eye, and the creamy mixture is not overly sweet and is pleasing to the palate.

INGREDIENTS

1 pint strawberries, cleaned and chopped
1/2 cup vanilla yogurt
3/4 chilled whipping cream
5 tablespoons sugar
1/4 cup orange juice
1 packet nonflavored gelatin
2 teaspoons orange liqueur
6 oranges, tops removed and hollowed out (or wineglasses)
strawberries for decoration

DIRECTIONS

Place strawberries in a bowl, slightly mash them, and drain.

Beat whipping cream into stiff peaks.

Mix together all the rest of the ingredients and mashed strawberries, and fold into whipped cream.

Divide and fill oranges (or wineglasses). When filling oranges, choose nice round oranges and scoop out the orange meat. If the orange is not standing with the opening on top, cut a slice off the bottom, allowing it to stand steadily.

Garnish with half strawberries and chill until served.

SUMMER PASTA SALAD

This is pasta salad that we would often serve at summer gatherings, many in our neighborhood. Neighborhoods are very special in Pittsburgh. Some neighborhoods are ethnic-based, like Polish Hill, Bloomfield, Homewood, and Squirrel Hill. They say Pittsburgh is a big city made up of hundreds of small neighborhoods. Quite true!

INGREDIENTS

For the salad:

- 4 cups spiral pasta, cooked and drained
- 1 can chickpeas, drained
- 1 cup cherry tomatoes cut in half (if large)
- 1 green pepper, diced
- 4 ounces mozzarella cheese, cut into strips
- 2/3 cup black olives, pitted and cut in half
- 2 ounces of salami or sopressata, cut into slices

For the dressing:

- 1/2 cup olive oil
- 1/3 cup red wine vinegar
- 1 teaspoon salt
- oregano and basil

DIRECTIONS

Cook pasta, and drain. Rinse lightly with cold water.
Combine all the ingredients together with the pasta.
Prepare the dressing, and pour over pasta and toss.
Cover and chill for several hours or overnight.

SUNSHINE CARROTS

These are carrots that I can get my family to eat. When we think of sunshine, Pittsburgh would not come to mind. While the average number of sunny days in the United States is 205, Pittsburgh comes in with 160. We get more rain than Seattle. Last year, we set a record of 57.8 inches of rain in Pittsburgh. Better news is that we are on track to exceed that record this year. Come visit. Enjoy the city, but bring your galoshes!

INGREDIENTS

5 medium-sized carrots, sliced into 1-inch pieces
1 tablespoon sugar
3 tablespoons butter
3/4 cup orange juice
1 teaspoon cornstarch
1/4 teaspoon ginger
1/4 teaspoon salt

DIRECTIONS

Steam the sliced carrots until tender (about twenty minutes). Remove to a serving dish and keep warm.

In a small saucepan, combine sugar, cornstarch, ginger, and salt.

Add the orange juice and cook. Stir constantly until the mixture bubbles and thickens. Allow to boil for one full minute.

Stir in the butter to finish the sauce, and pour over the carrots. Toss to coat the carrots evenly.

Serve warm.

TOMATO CAKES

I found this recipe in my ZiaZia's book. I make it in the summer when the tomatoes are fresh and sweet. Tomato cakes are a match with most main courses. I know Uncle Tony grew an abundance of tomatoes each summer, and ZiaZia was always trying new recipes for tomatoes.

INGREDIENTS

3 cups chopped tomatoes
3/4 cup flour and 3/4 teaspoon baking powder, sifted together
1 tablespoon sugar
salt and pepper to taste
3–4 tablespoons butter

DIRECTIONS

Mix the tomatoes and the rest of the ingredients to form a batter.
Heat butter in a fry pan. Drop spoonfuls of the batter into the heated butter, and fry.
Drain and serve immediately.

ZUCCHINI FRITTERS

Pittsburghers love their gardens, and many have zucchinis—more zucchinis than they know what to do with! Many use the zucchini to make bread. They bake it, or they fry it. I even once tasted a mock apple pie made of zucchini. This is one of the ways my Italian family made their zucchini. Fritters are always welcome!

INGREDIENTS

1 pound zucchini, shredded to 4 cups
2 eggs, separated
1/2 cup water
1/2 cup flour
1/4 teaspoon salt
1/4 cup onion, finely chopped
2 tablespoons Italian parsley, chopped
1/2 teaspoon basil, chopped
1 clove garlic, minced
3 tablespoons grated Romano cheese

DIRECTIONS

Place the 4 cups of zucchini in a bowl.

In another bowl, place the egg whites, and beat until stiff peaks are formed.

In still another bowl, place the egg yolks, and add water, flour, cheese, and seasonings. Beat this mix by hand.

Add the egg yolk mixture to the shredded zucchini, and then fold in the egg whites.

Add oil to a skillet, and heat to moderate heat.

Fry each fritter until golden brown.

Rest and drain on paper towels, and serve.

ZUCCHINI STUFFING CASSEROLE

This is a wonderful recipe; one of those that you read and then just have to make. It's a good use of zucchini. You could microwave the zucchini until tender, but I stopped microwaving about fifteen years ago. I guess the problem came when I decided to use the timer on the microwave. I thought it was great. On Memorial Day 1997, I chose to set that timer for 15 minutes while I made eggs. Problem was, I hit the cook button instead. I can't even imagine how it didn't catch on fire. I ran to get Les. He was very understanding. Then on Labor Day that same year, I did it again! He was not so understanding… But that Christmas, I got a very nice plastic timer shaped like a tomato. I use it to this day!

INGREDIENTS

4 medium zucchini sliced into 1/2-inch slices
7 tablespoons butter
3/4 cup sliced carrots
1 onion, chopped
2 1/2 cups stuffing cubes
1 can cream-of-chicken soup
1/2 cup sour cream

DIRECTIONS

Cook the zucchini slices in salted water until they are tender. Allow to drain.

In a 4-quart saucepan, melt 4 tablespoons butter. Add onions and carrots, and sauté until tender. Remove the pan from the heat, and empty the contents into a large bowl.

Then stir in 1 1/2 cups of the stuffing cubes, soup, and sour cream. Gently stir in the zucchini, and place in a casserole.

Melt the remaining butter in a skillet, and add the remaining stuffing cubes. Toss and top the casserole with the buttered stuffing cubes.

Bake at 350 degrees for 35–40 minutes.

PITTSBURGH CATHOLIC CHURCHES

I was raised Catholic. During the influx of immigrants into Pittsburgh, many families lived in the towns surrounding the steel mills. The Diocese of Pittsburgh made an effort to have churches of individual nationalities in the areas around the mills. This allowed the parishioners to attend Mass spoken in their own language. My mom's Italian family lived in Braddock and went to the Italian church, Our Lady of Mount Carmel. My cousin, Anthony DiVittorio, was the organist, and I remember the Italian priest who often visited the family home on Sundays after Mass. In Braddock, there was also the Polish church, Sacred Heart; the Slovak church, Saint Michael's; the German church, Saint Joseph; the Irish churches, Saint Brendan and Saint Thomas; and the Lithuanian church, Saint Isadore. After World War II, there was an effort to have the larger parishes build schools. The schools were affordable, and many nuns filled the teaching and administrative positions.

We lived in Eastmont, an eastern suburb of Pittsburgh. My brother Tom went to Saint Bartholomew School in Penn Hills. Not exactly sure why I wasn't allowed to go to a Catholic school, and I often questioned it. But nonetheless, every Saturday, while he slept in, I walked to the bus to go to catechism. I often passed the kids in the neighborhood going to Hebrew school, which made me feel a little better. We "bought" several pagan babies with quarters we would collect. I find it odd that we as a class would name the baby… It just seemed wrong for a group of nine-year-olds to name a baby. But I was so happy when we named one baby Matthew, a favorite name of mine.

Being Catholic, I didn't eat meat on Friday, didn't go into church without a covering on my head (even if it was only a tissue), genuflected at the pew, and never ate within an hour of Communion. My dad would yell up the stairs, "Eat now! It's nine thirty. Communion is in an hour!" I found it not so funny when I was going into a movie theater with my friends and absentmindedly forgot it wasn't a church and genuflected at the row before I went in. It took a good half hour for them to stop making fun of me!

I miss those days. Things in the Catholic church now are different. While they are more "user-friendly," somehow, I miss all the expectations and rules… Well, maybe except having to bobby-pin a tissue to my head!

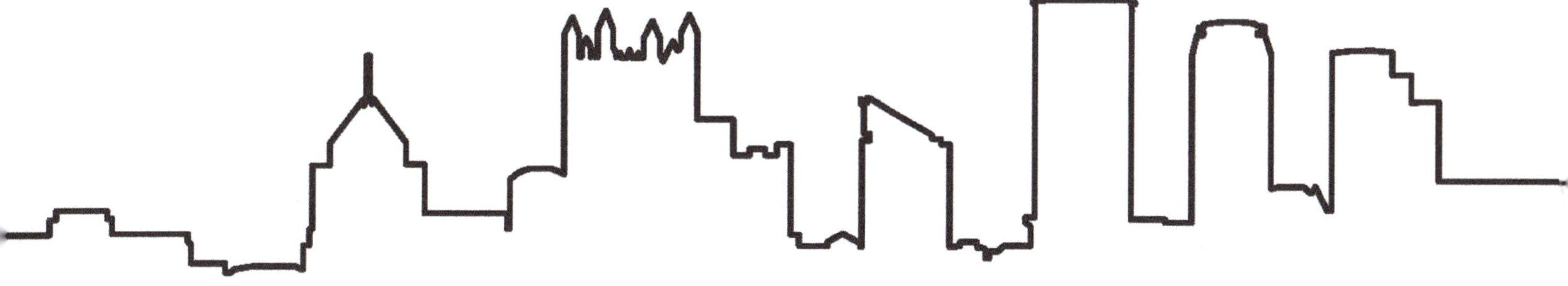

MAIN COURSES

APRICOT-GLAZED CHICKEN

Chicken drumsticks are a good, inexpensive meal when you feed a big family. It's not unusual to know many families in Pittsburgh with lots of children. Six or seven was the usual. The most I ever knew was one family that had thirteen kids. I grew up and went to church and school with an Irish family that had eight kids. The five girls all were named Mary something! We knew of another family where all the boys were a Bert—Albert, Norbert, Herbert, Egbert, and Gilbert!

INGREDIENTS

2 large shallots, finely chopped
16 ounces apricot preserves
1/4 cup ginger, peeled and finely chopped
1/4 cup honey
2 tablespoons oil
1/4 cup brown sugar, packed
1/2 cup red wine vinegar
1/3 cup soy sauce
16 chicken drumsticks
crushed red pepper to taste (optional)

DIRECTIONS

Cook the shallots and ginger until soft and golden. Stir in vinegar, and allow to boil until the mixture reduces by half (about 2 minutes). Add the honey, brown sugar, soy sauce, and apricot preserves. Cook this for 15 minutes.

Using an immersion blender, pulse to blend the sauce. Allow the sauce to cool.

Put the chicken legs in a container, and pour the marinade over them. Allow to marinate for 8 hours in the refrigerator.

Line a baking sheet with aluminum foil, and lightly grease. Arrange chicken, and brush with marinade. Discard remaining marinade since it has been exposed to raw chicken.

Bake in a 425-degree oven for 40 minutes, turning once.

BAKED EGGPLANT DINNER

This is one of those layered lasagna dishes, but names can be deceiving. Pittsburgh has lots of neighborhoods where the names might be misleading, like Squirrel Hill. Really, we all have about the same number of squirrels, same for turtles in Turtle Creek. If you travel to Level Green, you will find it is actually a hill! Not sure if you can buy glass in Glassport, but I bet you can find plums in Plum Borough! And of course, if you are really not of this world, you could choose to live in Moon Township or Mars Borough! All these locales are actual suburbs of Pittsburgh.

INGREDIENTS

1 large eggplant, peeled, sliced, and soaked in salted water for 1 hour
2 pounds ground meat (your choice of beef, sausage, pork, or a mix)
2 beaten eggs
1 cup milk
flour seasoned with garlic, salt, and pepper
Italian spaghetti sauce
flat Italian parsley
Romano cheese
olive oil
3/4 cup of bread crumbs
1/3 cup of Romano cheese

DIRECTIONS

Press two or three eggplant slices between your palms to remove the excess salted water.

Combine the beaten eggs with the milk in a bowl.

Dredge each slice of eggplant first in the flour and then in the egg-and-milk mixture. Fry each slice in 1/2 inch of olive oil, and set aside to drain.

Cook, season, and drain the ground meat.

In a 9-by-13-inch dish, layer the eggplant, ground meat, sauce, parsley, and cheese. Repeat until the dish is full.

Combine the bread crumbs and Romano cheese, and use it to top the casserole.

Bake in a 350-degree oven for 30–40 minutes or until heated thoroughly.

BAKED HAM WITH CHUTNEY GLAZE

Easter in Pittsburgh means baked hams! My godparents, Frances and Jim DiSalvo (Aunt Babe and Uncle Jimmy), were famous for their hams. The golden crust on the grid work scoring was amazing. Aunt Babe always put rings of sweet pineapple on the outside, and it would roast to a picture-perfect crusty goodness. No matter when we visited, it always ended in hours of pinochle, peanuts, and laughter.

INGREDIENTS

1 half ham, bone in
6 garlic cloves
1 8-ounce jar mango chutney
1/2 cup Dijon mustard
1/4 cup orange juice and zest of 1 orange
1 cup dark brown sugar

DIRECTIONS

Prepare and score the ham, and set aside.

In a food processor, mince the garlic cloves. Add the remaining ingredients, and pulse until smooth.

Pour over the ham, and bake ham according to the directions set. (Usually ham cooks at a low oven: 325 degrees for 20 minutes per pound.)

BAKED MAPLE EGGS AND BACON

Such a tasty mix of flavors! Great addition for a quick breakfast or brunch platter.

INGREDIENTS

1 pound of bacon, cooked, drained, and broken into pieces
12 eggs
12 slices of white or potato bread
3/4 cup of maple syrup
1/2 cup butter

DIRECTIONS

In a small saucepan, heat the butter and syrup together until the butter is completely melted. Set aside.

With the crusts removed, flatten each piece of bread. Brush the outside of the bread with the butter syrup mixture, and press a slice fully into each cup of an ungreased muffin tin.

Generously brush the inside of each piece of bread in the muffin tin with the butter syrup mixture.

In each tin, place pieces of bacon, and carefully break an egg on top. Cover this with foil.

Bake in a 400-degree oven for 18 to 20 minutes or until the eggs come to the desired doneness.

Serve immediately.

BAKED RIGATONI AND SAUSAGE

My Italian family didn't often mix meat with their pasta. Our Sunday dinners included spaghetti with a very thin tomato sauce. The meat was there, but always on the side. My mother would call those who made a meat sauce Medigan (American!), which in her southern Italian dialect meant *not* Italian and *not* in a very nice way!

INGREDIENTS

1 pound loose hot or sweet Italian sausage, cooked and drained
1/2 cup chopped onion
1 clove of garlic, minced
8 ounces small rigatoni, uncooked
1 cup ricotta
4 cups spaghetti sauce
2 cups shredded mozzarella
3 tablespoons Parmesan or Romano cheese

DIRECTIONS

Sauté loose sausage. When cooked, add the onions and garlic, and cook until the onion is tender.

In a separate pot, cook and drain the rigatoni according to package directions.

Combine the rigatoni, sausage, and ricotta.

In a casserole dish, pour 1/2 cup of spaghetti sauce on the bottom. Spread 1/3 of the sausage rigatoni mix on top. Cover with sauce and Mozzarella and Romano cheese. Repeat layering.

Bake at 400 degrees for 25 to 30 minutes or until hot and bubbly.

BAKED SOLE

Many Pittsburghers are Catholic (Roman or Orthodox), which back in the day meant *every* Friday you ate no meat. I have to say fish sticks had a very warm spot in my heart. Making them swim in ketchup (obviously that was made in Pittsburgh) made the experience even better! It became important to think of new ways to cook fish. This was a very fresh taste!

INGREDIENTS

2 pounds sole fillets
1 teaspoon salt
1/2 teaspoon pepper
1/2 cup dry vermouth
2 tablespoons lemon juice
3 tablespoons minced onion
1/4 pound sliced mushrooms
4 tablespoon butter
6 lemon wedges
flat Italian parsley to garnish

DIRECTIONS

Season the fish fillets with salt and pepper. Place fish in a greased baking dish.

In a bowl, mix vermouth, 2 tablespoons of melted butter, and lemon juice, and pour over the fish.

In a separate pan, sauté the mushrooms and onions in 2 tablespoons of butter, and place mix around the fish.

Bake in a 350-degree oven for 20 to 30 minutes or until the fish is fully cooked.

Garnish with lemon wedges and parsley, and serve.

BEEF STROGANOFF

Being Italian, I thought beef stroganoff was quite exotic. It was such an iconic flavor unlike any other in my little world. We never had fresh mushrooms. Actually, I am not even sure that our grocer offered anything but jars of mushrooms! However, I knew it was a good day when I saw the container of sour cream on the counter. It was either onion dip or beef stroganoff for dinner. Either way, I would be happy!

INGREDIENTS

1 1/2 pound round steak, cut into cubes and dusted with seasoned flour
pint of sliced fresh mushrooms
1 medium to large onion, sliced
3 tablespoons butter
1 can of beef consommé plus 1 can water
1 teaspoon Worcestershire sauce
1 cup sour cream
1 pound egg noodles, cooked and drained

DIRECTIONS

Melt butter in a large skillet, and sauté the mushrooms. Remove and set aside.

Add the onions and sauté until lightly browned. Remove and set aside.

Brown the floured beef cubes slowly. When browned, add the onions, mushrooms, beef consommé, water, and Worcestershire sauce. Cover the skillet, and allow to cook on medium to low for 1 1/2 hours.

Just before serving, gently mix in the sour cream and heat through.

Spoon stroganoff over egg noodles, and serve.

CABBAGE ROLLS
(GOLABKI, STUFFED CABBAGE, PIGS IN A BLANKET, HALUPKI)

Although this is a very Polish dish, most ethnic families make these for holidays, weddings, graduations, etc. My dad used to call them Polish hand grenades. They are loved and a staple of Pittsburgh ethnic cuisine. I was able to put this recipe together with the help of Les's cousins Suzy and Mike Bujakowski. Mike's mom, Adelia, was Polish and always put a bit of applesauce in her cabbage roll meat.

INGREDIENTS

1 1/2 pounds ground beef
1 1/2 pounds ground pork
1 1/2 cups uncooked rice
2 eggs, lightly beaten
1 teaspoon garlic powder
1 teaspoon salt
1/4 cup finely chopped onion
1 can of tomato soup
1/4 cup white or cider vinegar
1/2 cup applesauce
2 1/2 tablespoons sugar
2 heads cabbage, core removed

sauce
2–3 large cans of tomato soup

DIRECTIONS

Remove the core from the cabbage, leaving the cabbage leaves intact.

Fill a large pot with water, and place the cored cabbage in the pot. Allow it to cook until it is pliable.

In the meantime, combine the rest of the ingredients (except the 2–3 large cans of tomato soup) as you would a meat loaf. Set aside.

As the cabbage cooks, using tongs, slide each leaf off and allow to drain in a colander. Once the leaves are cool enough to handle, take an individual leaf with the center rib side up, and slice a small V so that you can remove that thick rib in the center. Turn the leaf over.

continued

Take a handful of meat—the size that will fit the leaf—and shape it into a hand grenade. Place the meat into the center, fold the sides, and roll the cabbage around the meat.

Whether you use a roaster, pan, or crock, spoon tomato soup on the bottom and alternately layer the rolls seam side down.

Cover the rolls with tomato soup, and repeat until finished.

Bake in a 350-degree oven for 1 1/2 hours.

CARAMEL FRENCH TOAST BAKE

This is "heaven on a dish." You can change the bread depending on the taste you desire. It is stunning when flipped onto a serving platter and those golden caramelized pecans or walnuts are a glowing, sticky nut cluster.

INGREDIENTS

2 loaves of cinnamon bread (18 slices)
1 1/3 cup brown sugar
3 tablespoons light corn syrup
3/4 stick butter
7 eggs
4 cups half and half
1/3 cup sugar
1 teaspoon vanilla
1 cup chopped pecans or walnuts

DIRECTIONS

Preheat oven to 350 degrees.

Put butter in a 9-by-13-inch pan, and place in oven. Allow to melt and remove. Spread the brown sugar in the pan, and drizzle the corn syrup over the butter-and-brown-sugar mix. Then spread the nuts into the mix.

Make 3 rows horizontally with the bread. Each row will have 6 slices. The bread should lean so that the top of the bread is level with the top edge of the pan.

Beat together the eggs, half and half, sugar, and vanilla, and pour the mixture over the bread.

Cover tightly with foil and refrigerate overnight.

Bake 1 hour covered, and 15 minutes more uncovered (place pan on foil or a cookie sheet in case there is overflow).

Remove from oven, and allow to rest for 5 minutes. Carefully invert on to a serving platter or cookie sheet, and serve.

CHAMPAGNE SHRIMP

Champagne and shrimp make a wonderful pairing. The shrimp marinates very well, and the recipe is simple. It's wonderful for a party menu or a Sunday brunch!

INGREDIENTS

For the sauce:

- 2 cups champagne
- 2 tablespoons champagne vinegar
- 1/2 cup finely chopped shallots
- 1/4 teaspoon black pepper

For the marinade and shrimp:

- 1 cup champagne
- 1/4 cup olive oil
- 3 tablespoons minced shallots
- 1/2 teaspoon black pepper
- 1 teaspoon minced straight parsley
- 1/2 teaspoon minced tarragon
- 1/2 teaspoon minced chives
- 24 extra large shrimp

For last addition to the sauce:

- 1 cup chilled butter

DIRECTIONS

Combine the sauce ingredients in a heavy saucepan. Bring to a boil, and allow reducing to about 1/4 cup or for about twenty minutes. Cover and allow to stand at room temperature.

Combine the ingredients for the marinade. Marinate shrimp for 30 minutes to an hour. Remove shrimp from marinade, and discard the marinade. Broil shrimp until cooked. Do not overcook.

Rewarm the sauce, and add the cup of butter. Allow the sauce to cook on low temperature. Do not allow the sauce to boil as it will separate.

Pour sauce over shrimp, and serve.

CHICKEN-AND-LEEK STRATA

Leeks are a flavorful addition to any dish. Make sure you clean your leeks, and drain them before sautéing them. This is comfort food at its best.

INGREDIENTS

2 tablespoons butter
2 cups leeks, cleaned and chopped
24 slices of French bread
2 cups cooked chicken, chopped
3 cups shredded mozzarella cheese
1 shallot, chopped
2 teaspoons dill
8 beaten eggs
4 cups milk
salt and pepper to taste

DIRECTIONS

Melt butter in a sauté pan. Add the leeks and shallot, and allow to cook until tender. Remove pan from the heat.

Line the bottom of a 13-by-9-inch dish with 1/2 of the bread slices.

Mix the leek-and-shallot mixture, chicken, dill, two cups of the mozzarella, and salt and pepper. Layer the chicken mixture over the bread slices. Top with the remaining bread and cheese.

Mix together the beaten eggs and milk, and pour over the casserole.

Cover tightly, and refrigerate overnight.

Bake in a 325-degree oven for 1 hour or until a knife inserted in the center comes out clean and hot.

Let stand 10 minutes, and serve.

CHICKEN CACCIATORE WITH PASTA

When I think of this recipe, I think of my great aunts wearing their babushkas and the tissues they always kept in their bosoms. It seemed to be a never-ending supply! There was the rare occasion when one of my aunts would get to church without their babushka. Luckily, they always had a hankie in their purse next to their rosary beads and a bobby pin to keep it on their head through Mass. The very last resort was that plastic folded rain bonnet that every woman carried in her purse but vowed never to use!

INGREDIENTS

2 tablespoons oil
2 cloves garlic
5 pounds of chicken pieces
2 medium onions, sliced
1 large can diced tomatoes
1 large can tomato sauce
1 teaspoon salt
2 teaspoons sugar
1/2 teaspoon oregano
1 bay leaf
1/2 pound spaghetti
Romano cheese

DIRECTIONS

In a large skillet, heat oil, and sauté the garlic. Remove the garlic, and brown chicken.

Once browned, remove the chicken, and to the skillet and drippings, add the onions. Sauté the onions until golden, stirring occasionally.

Add the tomatoes, tomato sauce, salt, sugar, and seasonings. Cook for 5 minutes.

Add the chicken back into the pan, cover, and allow to simmer for 50 minutes. Chicken should be tender.

Discard the bay leaf, and serve over spaghetti.

Sprinkle with Romano cheese.

CHICKEN SALTIMBOCCA

Pittsburgh is blessed with neighborhoods known for their ethnic residents. This recipe is from the Little Italy section—Bloomfield, just a stone's throw from Polish Hill!

INGREDIENTS

4 boneless chicken breasts
4 slices of prosciutto
4 slices of mozzarella cheese
1 tomato, sliced very thin
pinch of sage
bread crumbs for coating
2 tablespoons Italian flat parsley
2 tablespoons Parmesan cheese
3/4 cup butter, melted
salt and pepper to taste

DIRECTIONS

Pound each chicken breast between wax paper until flat.

On each breast, layer the prosciutto, mozzarella cheese, and tomato. Season each with salt and pepper and a pinch of sage, and roll like a jelly roll.

Secure each breast roll with a toothpick. Roll each breast in melted butter, and coat with bread crumbs. Season each breast with the parsley and Parmesan cheese.

Bake at 350 degrees for 45 to 50 minutes or until done.

SHRIMP-AND-CRAWFISH ÉTOUFFEÉ

I have to admit, it is a rare occasion to find crawfish in Pittsburgh! However, the local box store sells a frozen package of crawfish tail meat, and I could not resist using them to make an étoufeé. It is also a rare occasion to find étoufeé on a Pittsburgh menu!

INGREDIENTS

1/2 cup butter
1 large onion, chopped
2 ribs of celery, chopped
4 various colored peppers, chopped
3 cloves garlic, minced
2/3 cup flour
1 teaspoon salt
6 cups chicken stock
1 tablespoon Worcestershire sauce
2 tablespoon smoked paprika
2 teaspoons lemon juice
1 teaspoon sugar
1 tablespoon chopped parsley
1 teaspoon chopped chives

36 ounces crawfish tail meat
36 ounces shelled shrimp
cooked warm rice

DIRECTIONS

In a Dutch oven or pot, melt butter and add the onion, peppers and celery and sauté until softened. Add the minced garlic. Add the chicken stock and allow to cook on medium heat for 10 minutes. Put 1 cup of the chicken stock in a small bowl and whisk in the flour. Stir this mixture back into the pot. Add in the spices, sugar, Worcestershire Sauce and lemon juice and allow to cook for 2 minutes. Add the crawfish tail meat and the cleaned and shelled shrimp. Allow to cook on medium/low heat for 25 minutes.

Serve over warm rice and garnish with chopped scallions.

FRITZ'S SHRIMP-AND-SQUASH CASSEROLE

Our future son-in-law Ethan Ball's beloved grandfather's favorite dish. We have heard so many wonderful stories of Ethan's granddaddy! One of the finest cooks from the great state of Mississippi. The offer of good food and good conversation was always on his table!

Here's to you, Fritz Harris!

INGREDIENTS

3 pounds yellow squash, sliced thin
1 pound shrimp, cleaned and cut into bite-sized pieces
1 sleeve butter crackers
4 tablespoons butter
2 cups mild cheddar cheese + 1/4 cup cheddar cheese
1 tablespoon olive oil
salt, pepper, and garlic powder to taste

DIRECTIONS

Heat the olive oil in a pan, and sauté the squash until tender and set aside. Crush the crackers by hand. Melt the butter, and mix into the crackers.

In a 13-by-9-inch baking dish, layer the squash, shrimp, and cheese until the dish is full. Add salt, pepper, and garlic powder to each row to taste. Cover the top of the casserole with the buttered crackers, and then sprinkle 1/4 cup of cheese over the top.

Bake covered in a 350-degree oven for 30 to 35 minutes. Turn oven to 400 degrees, and continue to bake for an additional 10 to 15 minutes or until the top is golden brown.

Allow to rest for 10 minutes before serving.

GERMAN PANCAKE

My mom lived in a German section of Pittsburgh for a while. It is known as Deutschtown. Pittsburgh is home to one of the very few authentic German restaurants in the United States. It is the exact design as the original restaurant, which is actually located in Germany. It is a wonderful experience, both in the visual as well as culinary aspects. The band plays, lots of beer is served, and the long tables fill up every day! Close your eyes, and you will never know you are not in Germany!

INGREDIENTS

6 large eggs
1 cup whole milk
1 cup flour
1/2 cup sugar
1/2 teaspoon salt
3 tablespoon butter
confectioners' sugar

DIRECTIONS

Heat the oven to 400 degrees.

Beat together the eggs, milk, flour, sugar, and salt until frothy.

Melt the butter in a 10-inch cast-iron skillet. Remove the skillet with melted butter from the stove, and pour the egg mixture into the skillet.

Carefully place in the hot oven, and bake for 20 minutes or until golden and puffy.

Sift confectioners' sugar over the top, and serve immediately.

GRILLED OR BROILED LAMB CHOPS

These lamb chops are mouthwatering. The seasoning can be adjusted to individual tastes. I always include these on my brunch menus. We have been to many Pittsburgh weddings and bridal showers where these were the culinary highlight of the day. They are best grilled!

INGREDIENTS

20–25 lamb chops
1 tablespoon cinnamon
2 teaspoon coriander
2 teaspoons cumin
1/4 teaspoon ground clove
1/4 cup paprika
1/2 teaspoon cayenne
3 cloves garlic, Minced
I cup chopped Italian parsley
1 cup olive oil

DIRECTIONS

Mix all the ingredients together to form a marinade. Place the lamb chops in the marinade. Allow chops to marinate for at least 2 hours to overnight in the refrigerator.

Remove the lamb chops, and season with salt and pepper. Discard the marinade.

Grill or broil the chops until the lamb reaches 145 degrees.

Serve warm or at room temperature.

HOMEMADE GYROS

Pittsburgh is home to many people of Greek descent. The Greek Orthodox churches always have annual food festivals. Not only do the parishioners cook for months to prepare, but various other churches send members to work together at each other's festivals. These feasts are extremely well attended and are worth the wait in line.

INGREDIENTS

1 1/2 to 2 pounds of lamb stew meat
1 medium onion, chopped fine
1 teaspoon garlic, or 1 clove garlic, minced
1 teaspoon oregano
2 teaspoons kosher salt
soft pitas
tzatziki sauce

DIRECTIONS

Preheat oven to 300 degrees.

Place half of the lamb stew meat in a food processor with half of the onion and seasonings. Pulse until ground. Add the rest of the meat, and allow to process until very fine. Place in a bowl, and with moist hands, shape into a loaf. The loaf should be a rectangle—about 2 inches (height) by 5 inches (width) by 8 inches (length).

Bake until the internal temperature reaches 165 degrees.

Allow loaf to rest for 20 minutes, and slice into 1/4 inch slices. Place slices on a foil-lined cookie sheet. Broil for 4 minutes or until just crisping on the sides. Do not overbroil.

Assemble gyros by warming a soft pita and stuffing it with four or more slices of the warm gyro meat. Add large narrow slices of tomatoes, cucumbers, and onions. Add the tzatziki sauce. Wrap the gyro in foil square, making a triangle with the top open and the bottom secured so the gyro can be held and enjoyed.

HOT/SWEET SAUSAGE-STUFFED CABANA PEPPERS

I grew up going to our family (Capezzuto) house every Sunday for dinner. It was served after the noon Mass. It was always spaghetti with a thin tomato sauce. Meatballs, sausage, and these peppers were often on the side. The men sat in the dining room. The women sat at the very large round table in the kitchen. I was thrilled to sit on the chair from the mangle due to the shortage of chairs in the kitchen. It was pure love. (By the way, a mangle is a desk-like roller/presser for clothes. It was very popular in the forties.) That mangle chair now resides in my kitchen.

INGREDIENTS

Main ingredients:

- 6–8 large Cubanelle or hot peppers, tops removed and seeded
- 3–4 cups of spaghetti sauce

For the stuffing:

- 1 pound loose hot sausage
- 1 pound loose sweet sausage
- 1 1/2 cups seasoned bread crumbs
- 1/2–3/4 cup grated Romano cheese
- 1 1/2 teaspoon coarse salt
- 1 large shallot, diced
- 2 large eggs
- fresh parsley, chopped

DIRECTIONS

Combine all the stuffing ingredients in a bowl. Mix by hand until all ingredients are incorporated. Carefully fill each pepper with the stuffing.

In a large skillet, pour oil until the bottom of the pan has about 1/8 inch of oil. Heat and place peppers on their sides. Slowly cook the peppers, turning to each side. When peppers are browned and the stuffing is cooked, remove the peppers, and drain oil from the skillet.

Pour spaghetti sauce into the skillet, and allow the peppers to cook in the sauce on medium to low heat for about 30 minutes.

HUNGARIAN GOULASH

Pittsburgh has the ninth largest Hungarian population in the United States. There are many Hungarian restaurants around the Pittsburgh area. The goulash they serve is highlighted by rich, smoky paprika. It makes the dish pop with flavor.

INGREDIENTS

1 large onion, finely chopped
1 large red sweet pepper, finely chopped
1/2 cup butter
2 tablespoons paprika
1/2 teaspoon black pepper
2 cups beef stock
2 pounds beef, cut into 1 1/2-inch cubes
1 1/2 teaspoons salt
2 teaspoons cider vinegar

DIRECTIONS

In a Dutch oven, sauté the chopped onion and sweet pepper in butter. When the onion and pepper appear pale, remove and set aside.

Place the beef pieces in the Dutch oven, using medium to high heat, and allow to brown on all sides. Reduce the heat to low. Add the paprika, and stir until all the beef pieces are coated. Return the onion and peppers to the pot, and add the remaining ingredients. Simmer for 1 1/2 hours, stirring occasionally.

Serve over buttered noodles.

IMITATION CRAB PASTA

Imitation crab is quite versatile. It is made up of a variety of fish and really has a sweet taste. It is less expensive than the real crab and offers lower calories and sodium.

INGREDIENTS

24 ounces of imitation crab
1 large onion, chopped
2 cloves garlic, minced
1/2 cup olive oil
1 tablespoon capers
3 cups milk
1 1/2 cups Parmesan cheese
1 pound spaghetti, cooked and drained

DIRECTIONS

Sauté garlic and onions in the oil until transparent.
Break the crab into pieces, add to the mix, and allow to cook.
Add the capers. Add the milk and Parmesan cheese, and allow to cook until thickened.
Cook the spaghetti, and drain.
Mix crab mixture into the pasta, and serve warm.

ITALIAN COUNTRY PIE

My great-grandparents rented a farm in Trafford, Pennsylvania. My great-grandfather loved farming. Grandma, not so much! When she'd had enough, she headed back to Braddock, Pennsylvania, and refused to return. Grandpap and the six children followed, and our family homestead was established—213 Camp Avenue, Braddock. We would forever refer to it as "going down the house." We all used the back door, as we were family. The house was always filled with family, friends, food, laughter, and wonderful memories.

INGREDIENTS

For the crust:

- 1/2 cup tomato sauce
- 1/2 cup bread crumbs
- 1 pound ground meat or sausage, cooked and drained
- 1/3 cup chopped onions
- 1/3 cup chopped green peppers
- 1/4 teaspoon oregano
- salt and pepper to taste

For the filling:

- 1 1/3 cup cooked rice
- 1 1/2 cup tomato sauce
- 1/2 teaspoon salt
- 1 cup water
- 1 cup cheddar cheese

DIRECTIONS

Mix the crust ingredients, and press into a 9-inch pie plate.

Mix the filling with 1/2 cup of cheddar cheese. Spoon into the shell. Cover with foil and bake at 350 degrees for 25 minutes. Uncover and top with remaining cheese. Bake uncovered for an additional 15 minutes.

ITALIAN EASTER PIE

The Easter pie was always made by my cousin Anthony DiVittorio. He taught piano at Duquesne University. Often on summer afternoons, we would sit in the kitchen and listen to him play. Many of our family members are musically inclined. Anthony was so gifted that he took piano lessons at Carnegie Mellon University as a child. The family home had a grand piano in the living room next to the marble fireplace. It was such a beautiful room, and the music just enhanced it.

INGREDIENTS

1/2 pound loose hot sausage, cooked and drained
1 small onion, chopped
1/4 pound pepperoni, chopped
1/4 pound sopressatta or Italian salami, chopped
1/4 pound prosciutto, chopped
1 pound basket cheese, drained
1/4 pound mozzarella cheese, shredded
1/4 pound provolone cheese, shredded
1 pound ricotta
1/4 cup Parmesan cheese
1 cup sour cream
3 eggs, lightly beaten
black pepper to taste
2 9-inch pie crusts

DIRECTIONS

Cook the sausage. Add onions, and allow to cook. Drain the basket cheese and ricotta. Cut cheese into bite-sized pieces. Mix all ingredients together, and pack into the two pie crusts.

Bake at 350 degrees for 45 to 50 minutes.

Note: Basket cheese can be purchased at any Italian market. It is often available in the spring during the Easter season.

ITALIAN MEATBALLS

Meatballs—they are all made differently. Like pasta e fagioli, everyone has their way of making them. Some are large, some are medium, and the ones in wedding soup are tiny. I was never comfortable wetting and squeezing bread, but it had to be done. Many restaurants in Pittsburgh offer a meatball hoagie and homemade meatballs with their spaghetti.

INGREDIENTS

2 pounds ground meat
1 clove of garlic, minced
1/4 cup chopped parsley
6 slices dry bread, wet, squeezed, and torn into pieces
3/4 cup Romano cheese
salt and pepper to taste

DIRECTIONS

Put all ingredients into a large mixing bowl. Add 1 tablespoon olive oil, and add water 1 tablespoon at a time to form a workable mixture. Mix together, and refrigerate for 2 hours. Shape into balls.

In a large skillet, fry in 2 tablespoons oil or bake at 375 degrees on a cookie sheet.

JULI'S CROCK-POT SWEET HEAT CHICKEN

I could not ask for a more perfect daughter. She is smart, beautiful, funny, and boy, can that girl cook!

INGREDIENTS

4–6 chicken thighs, bone in and skin on
1/3 cup brown sugar
salt and pepper to taste
4 cloves of garlic
2 tablespoons flour
sriracha sauce

DIRECTIONS

Pat chicken dry, and add salt and pepper to each piece. Place skin side up in the Crock-Pot and turn Crock-Pot to high setting.

Sprinkle the brown sugar and minced garlic over the chicken. Drizzle the sriracha sauce over the chicken. Use the amount of sauce to reach the level of heat to taste.

Cook on the high setting for three hours. Turn the chicken over halfway through the cooking. When fully cooked, remove chicken from the pot, and set aside. Add the flour to the remaining liquid, and stir until a thick sauce is formed.

Place chicken on a bed of rice, and serve with the sauce.

KIELBASA STEW

Kielbasa is a staple for Pittsburgh. Many people are of Polish descent, and most butcher shops offer their own kielbasa. My husband Les's family makes fresh kielbasa. It is quite the event. There are, of course, the ingredients that his sister, Marlene, controls. The casings are washed, and the meat is cut and ground in a sausage stuffing machine powered by an old washing machine motor attached to a fan belt and two pulleys, all secured to a work bench. Who wouldn't have a blast making fresh kielbasa in a Pittsburgh basement!

INGREDIENTS

10–12 medium red potatoes, cut in 2-inch pieces
2 large white onions, cut into wedges
2 green peppers, seeded and cut into 2-inch pieces
2 pounds kielbasa, cut into 1-inch slices
1/2 cup oil
1 tablespoon basil and oregano
2 teaspoon salt and 1 teaspoon black pepper
1 pint heavy cream or half-and-half or whole milk
3 tablespoon cornstarch
3 tablespoon cold water

DIRECTIONS

In a roaster, place the potatoes, onions, peppers, and kielbasa. Combine the oil and seasonings, and pour over the vegetables and meat. Toss gently.

Cover the roaster, and bake at 350 degrees for 45 minutes. Stir occasionally.

Add the heavy cream, and allow to cook and additional 45 minutes or until the potatoes are tender. When finished, place the roaster on the top of the stove.

Mix the cornstarch and cold water separately, and then add to the roaster. Bring to a boil, stirring constantly, allowing the stew to thicken.

LAMB PIE

Many cultures in Pittsburgh enjoy lamb. It is not as popular as beef and chicken, but it should not be overlooked. This pie honors my dad Howard's family (Lutton and McCall), which is Irish, Scotch, and English. I made this recipe for a local Irish restaurant as a potential new recipe for their menu. It is such a pleasant flavor and can be decorated to make a beautiful presentation.

INGREDIENTS

1 1/2 pounds lamb
1 pound onions (Bermuda, white, Vidalia, yellow)
1 large Granny Smith apple
1/4 teaspoon nutmeg
1/2 teaspoon allspice
1 cup beef stock
pie crusts, top and bottom
salt and pepper to taste

DIRECTIONS

Cut lamb into pieces, and sauté in olive oil.

Chop onions, and slice the apple.

In a large ceramic dish, layer the onions, meat, seasonings, spices, and apple. Repeat. Top with a pie crust. You can save small pieces of dough to decorate the top of your pie.

Bake for 1 hour to 1 hour and 15 minutes.

LEMON PEPPERED PASTA WITH TUNA AND ARUGULA

As a Roman Catholic in Pittsburgh, eating fish every Friday often meant that tuna noodle casserole made with mushroom soup was on the menu. Truthfully, it gets quite old after a while—a short while! We found these noodles as a specialty store, and the rest was history. I am a real fan of arugula, and it works well here, but you could use spinach or kale as well.

INGREDIENTS

1 large 12 ounce can of tuna, well drained
1/3 cup olive oil
1 medium onion, coarsely chopped
2 tablespoons capers
1 heaping handful of fresh arugula, spinach, or kale
1 tablespoon coarse salt
2 16-ounce packages of lemon peppered noodles
Romano cheese to taste

DIRECTIONS

Bring a large pot of well-salted water to a boil. Boil the pasta for 12 minutes. At about halfway through the boiling, add the handful of arugula to the pasta and allow to cook with the pasta.

In a large skillet, heat the olive oil. Add the chopped onion and capers. Sauté until the onions are transparent. Add the tuna. Add one tablespoon of coarse salt.

Drain the pasta and arugula, and place in serving bowl. Pour tuna mix over the pasta, and serve with Romano cheese.

LINGUINI ALFREDO

The Italian Order of Sons and Daughters is a national organization with over 20 million members, of which I am one. The Pittsburgh IOSD Chapter is one of the largest in the country. There is a richness to honoring your ethnic roots.

INGREDIENTS

1 pound egg noodles
1/2 cup butter
1 cup heavy cream
1 cup Parmesan cheese
1/3 cup Swiss cheese
salt and pepper to taste

DIRECTIONS

Cook egg noodles, and drain.

In a heavy medium-sized saucepan, melt the butter, and add the cream. Allow to cook. In a bowl, pour the butter and cream over the warm cooked pasta, and add the cheeses.

Toss and serve.

(Cooked chicken or cooked shrimp can be added to this dish.)

LINGUINI CON AGLIO E OLIO

There is a rich simplicity to this pasta. When you eat pasta at least once a week, it's nice to have a variety that is not with a red or thick white sauce. I especially love to use fresh parsley with this.

INGREDIENTS

1/3 cup olive oil
4 cloves of garlic, minced
1 can anchovy fillets, drained
1 pound linguini
3 tablespoon butter
1/4 teaspoon pepper
2 tablespoon Italian parsley, chopped
1/2 cup cooked pasta water
Romano or Parmesan cheese to finish

DIRECTIONS

Cook and drain linguini. Add the butter, pasta water, pepper, and parsley to the hot pasta, and set aside.

Heat oil in a skillet, and add anchovies and garlic. Allow this to cook. Add the anchovy sauce to the linguini, and serve.

Add Romano or Parmesan cheese if desired.

LINGUINI WITH WHITE CLAM SAUCE

Only true Italian restaurants will offer linguini with clam sauce. This is not always what you think of when you think of a spaghetti dish. But in Pittsburgh, many things aren't what you think. Our over 700 sets of stairs that have served the area are more than you would ever imagine. They allow access up and down the hills and were a mainstay during the height of the working mills. The longest set has 376 steps! Many of these steps are actually legal streets with names, and they are salted in the winter and pruned and swept in the summer. The South Side Slopes (obviously not a flat area) of Pittsburgh has the most sets of stairs. Can you imagine working an eight-hour shift in the mill and then walking up 376 stairs to get home!

INGREDIENTS

1 medium onion, chopped
1 clove garlic, minced
3 tablespoons olive oil
2 tablespoons butter
1/2 teaspoon oregano
1/2 cup Italian parsley, minced
1/3 cup white wine
2 cans (6 ounces) minced clams, undrained
salt and pepper to taste
1 pound linguini, cooked and drained

DIRECTIONS

In a heavy saucepan, heat the oil and butter. Sauté onion and garlic until tender, but do not allow to brown. Add the parsley and oregano, and allow to simmer for a few minutes. Add the white wine and clams, and cook about 20 minutes, allowing the alcohol to cook off. Season with salt and pepper.

Cook linguini and drain, but do not rinse. Pour the clams over the linguini, and serve.

LITTLE AL'S BIG SANDWICH

Little Al was my cousin. Such a great guy and lots of fun! He was a plumber and was in the same nursing home as my mom. They often would look out the nursing home window at the Italian food store across the street. They talked about the food they remembered, and this was a sandwich that he loved and missed being able to make. We have enjoyed it ever since. It is an event of a sandwich, perfect for gatherings and parties. Les and the kids always request this while watching hockey games.

<u>INGREDIENTS</u>

1 loaf of Italian bread
1/4–1/3 pound ham, sliced
1/4–1/3 pound sopressatta or salami, sliced
1/4–1/3 pound hot capicola ham, sliced
1/4–1/3 pound provolone cheese, sliced
1/2 head lettuce, cleaned and shredded
1/2 onion, thinly sliced
olive oil, red wine vinegar, oregano, parsley, salt, and pepper

<u>DIRECTIONS</u>

Cut the Italian bread horizontally lengthwise. On a cookie sheet, place the top piece of the bread facing up (crust down), and sprinkle with olive oil. Layer the meats and cheese on the bottom half of the loaf, and place on the cookie sheet next to the top half.

Bake at 375-degree oven until the meats and cheese are hot and the top of the bread is toasted.

Remove from the oven. Mix together the oil, vinegar, and spices as you would a salad dressing. Toss together with the lettuce and onions.

Place the prepared lettuce-and-onion mixture on top of the warmed meats and cheese. Replace the top of the loaf on top of the lettuce-and-onion mixture to reform the loaf.

Slice in thick slices (as you would a loaf of Italian bread), and serve warm.

MANDARIN-ORANGE-AND-CHICKEN SALAD

I put this salad together for Les, and we have enjoyed it ever since. I usually choose a sweet mayonnaise. The curry just makes the taste so unique and compelling. I often refer to Les as my Squirrel Man. He gathers, sorts, stores, and starts again. We had to provide the music for an event, and I threw this together because it took him sooo long to get things into the car. I guess there is a positive to waiting for the Squirrel Man to get moving!

INGREDIENTS

1 rotisserie chicken, cut and diced
1 large can mandarin orange, drained
1/2 cup sliced almonds, toasted
1 stalk celery, chopped
2 teaspoons curry powder
1 cup mayonnaise / tangy salad dressing

DIRECTIONS

Remove the meat, and chop into bite-sized pieces. Place in a large bowl. Drain mandarin oranges and coarsely chop. Add to the chicken. Toast the sliced almonds, and add to the bowl. Add the chopped celery. In a smaller bowl, mix the mayonnaise and curry together. When blended, add to the large bowl, and mix all ingredients together.

Keep refrigerated, and serve cold on crackers of your choice.

MANICOTTI

If there is a recipe that is truly my mom's, it's this one. She made this so well that I could not even think to try it. Her crepes were paper thin and so light. Her ricotta filling was the perfect addition to this delicate entrée. She normally served this with her spaghetti sauce, but on occasion, she would use a béchamel sauce. Many Italians in Pittsburgh don't always add that ending "I." So for much of my childhood, I thought these were called Minnecot! Call them what you like. They are the best comfort food I know!

INGREDIENTS

For the batter:

2 cups of milk
2 cups flour
9 eggs
pinch of salt

For the filling:

3 pounds ricotta (single recipe)
1 good handful of Italian cheese (Romano or Parmesan)
4 very large eggs
salt and pepper to taste
(1 pound of cooked and drained ground meat can be added)

DIRECTIONS

Combine all the ingredients for the filling in a bowl, and refrigerate overnight.

Beat together the ingredients for the batter. In a small to medium nonstick (or brushed with oil) skillet, make batter into crepes. In each crepe, place filling in the center, and fold both ends in, forming a tube.

Place the manicotti seam side down in a serving dish on a layer of spaghetti sauce. These should not be layered. Top with spaghetti sauce and Italian cheese.

Bake at 350 degrees for 25 minutes or until heated through.

MARIE'S EGGPLANT AND TOMATO PASTA

I need to pay homage to my Monday crochet club. The following is Marie Maruco's recipe. We are the Happy Hookers of Trafford, Pennsylvania. Judy Ference, Diane Kuntz, Marie Maruco, Lynn Palmer, Laverne Lokay, Nancy Shaw, Vicki Pirano, and Mary Jean Williams. We journey through life one stitch at a time. Our annual Christmas project is to make scarves and hats for the area children who use the Trafford Library. Our paths have put us together, and we are ever so blessed!

INGREDIENTS

2 cloves garlic, chopped
2 small eggplants, skin removed and chopped
1 pint of large cherry tomatoes, cut into quarters
3 tablespoon sugar
1 tablespoon chopped parsley
1/4 cup olive oil
1 pound penne pasta
Parmesan or Romano cheese

DIRECTIONS

In a large skillet, sauté garlic. Add chopped eggplant and cherry tomatoes, and continue until the eggplant is fully cooked. If needed, add more olive oil. Add the sugar and parsley, and allow to simmer.

Cook pasta and drain. Place pasta in a serving bowl, and pour the tomato-and-eggplant mix over it.

Serve immediately with Parmesan or Romano cheese.

PASTA À LA PADRINO

Many times, my family liked things spicy. Uncle Tony and Aunt Julie DiVittorio had a string of red peppers hanging in their large kitchen at the family homestead. It was such an amazing kitchen. The very large round table in the center drew visitors to sit. Coffee was always just a pour away, and a plate heaping with fresh biscotti made the many Italian conversations flow. I loved it when Italian was spoken. Such a memory!

INGREDIENTS

1 pound spaghetti or linguini
4 cloves garlic, minced
1 cup olive oil
2–4 red hot peppers, seeded and finely chopped
1/4 cup Italian flat parsley
1 cup Parmesan cheese
1 cup pasta water, if needed

DIRECTIONS

Sauté garlic and peppers. Cook pasta, and drain. Do *not* rinse. Return pasta to the pot, and pour the sautéed peppers and garlic over it. Add the cheese and parsley, and toss well. If the pasta seems dry, you can add some of the pasta water.

PASTA WITH KALE

This is a great quick dish. On a cold and wintry night, there's nothing like pasta! Pittsburgh offers a wide variety of weather. We have cold, snowy winters; hot, humid summers; and actually, more rain than Seattle, Washington! The temperature ranges are ridiculous. Most Yinzers joke that we can go through three seasons of weather in one day! *Yinzer* is an affectionate term that Pittsburghers use to refer to themselves. It comes from the use of the colloquialism *yinz* in conversation in place of *you*. Yinzers pride themselves in their ability to drive in snow and ice. Since Pittsburgh is located in the Appalachian Mountains, if you cannot navigate a steep grade up, down, and around a snow-covered street, you might as well move to the South!

INGREDIENTS

1 pound pasta
1 bunch kale or broccoli rabe, cleaned and cut into pieces
1 medium onion, chopped
1 red pepper, chopped
1 clove garlic, minced
1/2 cup olive oil
1/2 cup pasta water

DIRECTIONS

Boil the pasta in well-salted water. Right after you add the pasta, add the kale, and allow to cook with the pasta using the directions on the pasta box.

In a sauté pan, heat olive oil, and add the onion and pepper. Cook for 2 minutes, and add the garlic. Remove one half cup of the pasta water, and set aside. Drain the pasta and kale, but do *not* rinse.

Put the pasta and kale back into the pot, and pour the onion, pepper, and garlic mix over the pasta. If the mix seems to be dry, add a little of the pasta water. Mix and serve.

Many items can be added to this pasta—shrimp, cooked sausage, cooked chicken, or any vegetable(s) of choice.

POT STICKERS AND CHICKEN STIR-FRY

This is a throw-together dinner that I serve right out of a very large skillet. It's easy and tasty, and it's all done in that same skillet!

INGREDIENTS

1 bag (10–12 pieces) frozen chicken pot stickers
2–3 chicken breast strips, seasoned and cooked
1 clove garlic, minced
1 shallot, diced
1–2 medium onions, diced
1 small to medium head of cabbage, sliced
1 carrot, diced
1/3 cup olive oil plus some oil for browning the pot stickers
1/4–1/3 cup soy sauce
2–3 tablespoons brown sugar

DIRECTIONS

Drizzle a small amount of oil in a large skillet. Brown the pot stickers, and remove. Set aside.

Again, drizzle some oil in the skillet, and cook the chicken breast strips. Season with sea salt, pepper, and garlic. Once fully cooked, remove and set aside.

Add the 1/4 cup oil in the same skillet, and heat over medium setting. Add the minced garlic and the shallot. Allow to cook for 1–2 minutes. Add the onion and cabbage. Turn the heat setting to medium to high, and allow to cook until the cabbage becomes limp and browns slightly.

Once the cabbage mix is cooked, add the soy sauce and brown sugar. Allow this to mix and incorporate. Return the browned pot stickers and cooked chicken strips to the same skillet, and allow the dish to cook on low heat until you are ready to serve.

PUMPKIN SPICE WAFFLES

Western Pennsylvania is a large producer of maple syrup. Meyersdale, Pennsylvania, about one and a half hours from downtown Pittsburgh, has a yearly Maple Festival that celebrates everything maple. These are the waffles we make when we bring home that special hometown maple syrup!

INGREDIENTS

4 cups all-purpose flour
1/2 cup brown sugar
2 tablespoons baking powder
1 teaspoon salt
1 1/2 teaspoons cinnamon
1/2 teaspoon ginger
1/4 teaspoon nutmeg
4 eggs, lightly beaten
3 cups whole milk
1 can (15 ounces) canned pumpkin
1/3 cup melted butter

DIRECTIONS

Heat waffle iron. In a large bowl, mix the dry ingredients—flour, brown sugar, baking powder, and spices.

In another large bowl, mix the beaten eggs, milk, melted butter, and pumpkin. Take large spoonfuls of the wet mix, and add to the dry. Mix until incorporated, but do not overmix.

Bake in the waffle iron until done. Place finished waffles in warm oven until ready to serve.

QUICK AND EASY QUESADILLAS

Our kids—Jake, Adam, and Juli (or as some know them, Itchy, Scratchy, and Petunia)—love these. It's hard to believe how quickly they have grown. We love them more every day. Our family get-togethers are filled with laughter, love, and of course, *food*!

INGREDIENTS

1 pound chicken cut into strips, seasoned
4 cups shredded cheese, Monterrey Jack or cheddar
1 large onion, chopped
1–2 large red or green peppers
4 large tortillas
jalapenos, black olives, cooked black beans, etc. (optional)

DIRECTIONS

In a skillet, season and sauté chicken strips in a small amount of olive oil, and set aside. Sauté the onions and the peppers, and set aside as well.

In a large skillet over medium heat, lay the tortilla flat, and allow to warm so it is pliable. On one half of the tortilla, place a layer of shredded cheese. Next, place a layer of chicken, followed with a layer of sautéed onions and peppers. Put another layer of shredded cheese. Fold over the rest of the tortilla, and place a heavy plate or bacon/sandwich press. Allow the quesadilla to cook. After a couple of minutes, turn the quesadilla over, and allow the other side to cook.

Once the tortilla is golden brown, remove and serve.

RAVIOLI

My great-uncle Tony DiVittorio loved ravioli. He made our family home in Braddock a showplace. He was a plasterer, and even all the "wood moldings" in his house were made of plaster. He was so talented. Since our grandfather had died, he was like our Pap. I remember him making a little bunny out of his handkerchief and then magically making it jump up his arm. I often smell his cigars and so remember his strong Italian accent. He had an old truck that we loved. My brother, Tom and I knew that if we were riding and it rained, one of us had to manually work the windshield wipers with the little switch on the dashboard. We adored him and loved every minute that we spent with him!

INGREDIENTS

For the filling:

- 2 pound ground chuck
- 2 pounds ricotta
- salt and pepper to taste
- chopped parsley to taste
- 7 eggs
- 3/4 cups Romano cheese

For the ravioli dough:

- 10 cups flour
- 6 eggs
- 1/2 teaspoon salt
- A little water

DIRECTIONS

Sauté ground chuck, and drain. Add salt, pepper and parsley. Allow to cool.

When cool, add the ricotta, cheese, and eggs. Refrigerate overnight.

Next day, mix dough until it is elastic. Separate into two balls, and keep covered with a towel.

Using a pasta machine, roll the dough into thin long strips, about 3 inches wide. Place a dollop of the ricotta mix on the strip at about every 3 inches. Brush around each dollop with a small amount of water. Place a thin strip of dough identical to the first strip with the dollops on it on top of the first strip, and press around each dollop. Cut with a ravioli cutter.

This recipe can be made in half quantities. If freezing, freeze the uncooked ravioli individually spread on a cookie sheet. Once completely frozen, they can be stored in a freezer bag.

SAMMAS

Nicknames. My husband's German family and their nicknames! Puppy Muchitsch—we don't even know his real name. His boys were Dench and Moo. Big Yep, Little Yep—two friends both named Jake. Spike, a.k.a. Junior, worked on the railroad. WeeWee—we don't know why this poor woman carried the name WeeWee. Huntz and Honus are both German for John. Geebee, Grimes, Cookie, Puddin'—who doesn't love puddin'? Babe—how many Babes can you have? Women and men alike—we lost count! And one Babe was a fan dancer, a stripper no less, in East Pittsburgh!

This is a very German recipe. I was never able to find it in any search. It is from the Old Country and has been made every New Year's Eve with the celebratory pork and sauerkraut.

INGREDIENTS

3 pounds ground meat
1 cup raw white rice
1 medium chopped onion
1 teaspoon salt, pepper, and garlic

DIRECTIONS

Mix all ingredients together, and form into small balls.

Gently place each ball into the roaster filled with your pork roast and sauerkraut. These will cook as your pork roast cooks.

Be very careful not to damage these if you need to stir the roaster.

SATURDAY NIGHT SPECIAL

Sometimes a Saturday night needs a meal that sticks to your ribs. This is it! Pittsburgh eateries often like to stack food—sandwiches stacked with meat, fries, slaw, etc. This dish does just that, and the fried egg on the top is the best part!

INGREDIENTS

1 bag of hash browns or sliced potatoes
4 hamburger patties
2 cups cheddar cheese, grated
1–2 large onions, sliced
8 large eggs
salt and pepper to taste
oil for frying

DIRECTIONS

In a large skillet, fry the hash browns or potatoes until golden. Drain and set aside. Adding oil if needed, fry the onions, and set aside. In the same skillet, fry the meat, and set aside. Fry the eggs to sunny side up.

On each large dinner plate, stack a large spoon of the cooked hash browns, a hamburger patty, a spoonful of onions, and 1/2 cup of cheddar cheese. Top the stack with the 2 fried eggs.

This serves 4.

SHRIMP CREOLE

Pittsburgh, as a city, has received numerous culinary awards for its diversity, innovation, and variety. As much as Pittsburgh honors and embraces its ethnic roots, we are not afraid to step out of our comfort zones and try different tastes! Shrimp creole may not be home to Pittsburgh, but it is a great dish to warm your heart when a blustery cold day blows through town!

INGREDIENTS

1 large onion, chopped
3 peppers, red or green
2 cloves of garlic
3 tablespoons of vegetable oil
2 29-ounce cans diced tomatoes plus 1 can of water
2 29-ounce cans tomato sauce plus 1 can of water
1 large can tomato paste plus 2 cans of water
3 boxes of Spanish rice
2 pounds large uncooked shrimp, cleaned and shelled
2 tablespoons chili powder
3 tablespoons brown sugar

DIRECTIONS

In a large pot, heat vegetable oil, and sauté onions, garlic, and peppers until soft. Add the tomatoes and water. Add the chili powder and brown sugar. Allow to cook for 20 minutes.

Add the three boxes of Spanish rice, cover, and simmer for 45 minutes to an hour.

Add the shrimp, and continue to simmer for another 30 minutes.

SICILIAN MARINATED SAUCE

Some recipes you can say are the best. This is one. It is an excellent quick fresh sauce. No need to cook for hours. Many things in Pittsburgh are the "best" or "most." First, Pittsburgh has more bridges than any city in the world. That would be a whopping 446! Pittsburgh also boasts over 700 sets of outdoor stairs throughout the city—keeps us all in shape! And we can't forget that Pittsburgh has more bars per capita than another other city in the United States. I'll take a shot and a beer, please!

INGREDIENTS

2 tablespoons olive oil
1 large onion, chopped
1 clove garlic, smashed slightly
1 large can chopped tomatoes
1 large can of tomato sauce
1/3 cup Romano cheese
1 tablespoon chopped Italian parsley
1 tablespoon sugar
2 shots sweet vermouth
pinch of oregano

DIRECTIONS

In a large sauté pan, heat oil, and cook the onions and garlic until golden. Remove the onions and garlic from pan, saving the oil. Discard the onions and garlic.

Add the tomatoes, tomato sauce, and all the remaining ingredients except for the vermouth. Cook over medium to low heat for 1 hour. Add the vermouth, and allow to cook an additional 15 minutes.

Serve over pasta.

SPAGHETTI SAUCE

This recipe was my introduction to cooking. When my mom cooked this sauce each week, it was my job to push the tomatoes through the large colander. I remember standing on a chair to reach the counter and using my knuckles to push the tomatoes through. I learned very quickly that if I went too far, my knuckles would get skinned.

INGREDIENTS

small package country-style pork ribs
1 large onion, diced
1 large can whole tomatoes
1/3 cup Italian parsley
1 clove garlic, minced
2 teaspoons brown sugar
dash of salt
3 small cans tomato paste
1 large can tomato sauce

DIRECTIONS

In a large pot, add 2 tablespoons of oil and brown the meat. Once browned, add 1 large diced onion. Brown lightly. Add 1 large can of whole tomatoes that have been pushed through a sieve or blender. Add 1/3 cup fresh Italian parsley, I clove garlic (minced), 2 teaspoons of brown sugar, and a dash of salt. Cook this for 1 hour.

In a blender, place 3 small cans of tomato paste, fill each empty can with water, and add it to the blender. Add 1 large can of tomato sauce to the blender. Blend until incorporated, and add to the pot with the country-style ribs. Cover and cook for 2 hours. Taste for sugar, adding more if necessary.

If adding meatballs, place cooked meatballs into the sauce when you add the tomato paste and sauce. Allow to cook until the meatballs are heated through.

A handful of Romano cheese can be added when ready to serve over pasta.

STUFFED PEPPERS

My sister-in-law, Marlene, makes great stuffed peppers! Marlene had a Pittsburgh shower in her basement. Some people have a Pittsburgh toilet. Marlene opted for the shower. With six kids—Kim, Kevin, Kerry, Kenny, Kathy, and Karen—an extra shower was a good thing. This was a freestanding showerhead in the center of the basement, strategically located over a floor drain, surrounded with a shower curtain. No walls needed! You just can't imagine how many older homes in Pittsburgh have Pittsburgh toilets or showers. In their own way, they are classics.

INGREDIENTS

1 to 1 1/2 pounds of ground meat
4 large green bell peppers, washed, tops removed, and seeded
1 cup uncooked instant rice
2–3 large cans of tomato soup
1/2 cup chopped onion
1 teaspoon garlic powder
1 teaspoon salt
1/4 cup water

DIRECTIONS

Combine the ground meat, rice, salt, onion, garlic powder, one cup of tomato soup, and the water in a large bowl. Stuff each pepper with equal amounts of the ground-meat mixture. Put a layer of tomato soup on the bottom of a 13-by-9-inch baking dish. Pour the remaining tomato soup around the peppers.

Preheat oven to 350 degrees. Cover dish with foil, and cook for 45 to 60 minutes. Uncover and bake an additional 5 minutes. Internal temperature should reach 160 degrees before serving.

SUNDAY AFTERNOON CHICKEN STEW

I made this recipe hoping it would be like a country stew. It is a hearty Sunday meal for my family. I love to use my Dutch oven for meals like this and let it cook for hours.

INGREDIENTS

1–2 pounds of chicken, boneless or bone in
10 medium potatoes, washed cut into quarters
2 cloves garlic, whole
2 cups carrots, thickly sliced
2 medium onions, chopped
3 tablespoons butter
1/4 cup olive oil
4–6 cups chicken broth
1/4 cup butter
1/2 cup flour
1/2 cup heavy cream
1 teaspoon chopped parsley
1/2 teaspoon white pepper

DIRECTIONS

In a heavy skillet, melt 3 tablespoons of butter, and add 1/4 cup olive oil. When hot, brown chicken on all sides, and set aside. In a Dutch oven, place chopped onions, garlic, potatoes, carrots, parsley, and white pepper. When chicken is cool enough to handle, cut boneless chicken into thick medallions. If using bone in chicken, place chicken throughout the Dutch oven.

In a skillet, melt the 1/2 cup butter, and add the 1/2 cup flour forming a roux. Cook and add the chicken broth. Whisk until a thick sauce forms. Add the heavy cream, and stir until incorporated. Pour over the chicken and vegetables in the Dutch oven.

Cover and bake in a 350-degree oven for 1 1/2 hours.

SWEDISH MEATBALLS

I found this recipe in my great-aunt ZiaZia's book. It surprised me, but not as much as the Amish recipe for noodles and stewed tomatoes and my grandmother's recipe where you start with frozen round steak in a pan! I can't even imagine either of them making either one of those!

INGREDIENTS

1 pound ground chuck
1/2 pound ground pork
1/2 pound ground Veal
1 cup plain bread crumbs
1 cup milk
1 onion, minced
2 eggs, beaten
1/4 teaspoons nutmeg
3 tablespoons butter
1/4 teaspoon allspice
2 tablespoons oil
1/3 cup butter
1/3 cup flour
4 cups beef broth
pinch of grated lemon
salt and pepper to taste
1 cup sour cream
1 pound egg noodles

DIRECTIONS

Blend together the meats, bread crumbs, and milk. Do not overmix. Sauté the onion in 1 tablespoon of butter, and add to the meat mixture along with nutmeg, allspice, and salt and pepper to taste. Mix with hands to get an even texture, and form into small balls.

In the remaining 2 tablespoons of butter, brown the meatballs. When browned completely, remove from skillet, and add the 1/3 cup of butter to the pan drippings. Whisk in the flour to form a roux, and cook for a minute or two. Whisk in the broth, and cook until hot and taste for seasonings.

Return the meatballs to the skillet, and allow to simmer for 1 hour.

When ready to serve, cook egg noodles, and drain. Remove the meatballs from the sauce with a slotted spoon, and set aside. Add the sour cream and grated lemon to the sauce, and allow to heat through.

Return the meatballs to the sauce, and serve over egg noodles.

SWEET-MUSTARD HAM AND GLAZE

I have read that mustard was the first condiment put on food. It dates back to the pharaohs of Egypt. Today, most of our mustard is produced in Canada and Nepal. There is no end to the mixing of spices and acidic liquid to make so many varieties of mustard. This ham glaze is mustard at its best. Move over, hot dogs and ham sandwiches!

INGREDIENTS

4 cloves of garlic
1 8-ounce jar of mango chutney or mango jam
1/2 cup Dijon mustard
1/3 cup orange juice
1 cup light brown sugar
1 ham

DIRECTIONS

Mince garlic in a food processor. Add the mango chutney, mustard, orange juice, and brown sugar. Process this until smooth.

In the final hour of cooking, pour glaze over the ham, and allow to finish baking for 1 hour.

TENDERLOIN WITH MUSHROOM-AND-BACON DUXELLES

Invite the boss because this is the dish to serve! It is classy and is a picture on a platter!

INGREDIENTS

pork or beef loin or butterfly pork chops, cut for stuffing
6–8 slices of peppered bacon
1 pound mushrooms
1/2 cup chopped onion
1 tablespoon chopped flat parsley
salt and pepper, both the mushroom mix and meat
puff pastry, store bought
egg wash, 1 egg with 1 tablespoon of water added

DIRECTIONS

Sauté the bacon. Add the onions and mushrooms. Season the mix with salt, pepper, and the parsley. Cook this mixture until it is paste-like.

Stuff the tenderloin or chops with the mushroom mix. Wrap in puff pastry, using egg wash to seal the edges. If you can save just a small piece of pastry, it is nice to cut small leaves to decorate the top of the tenderloin.

Bake seam side down at 350 degrees for 40 minutes or more, depending on the doneness of the meat. All meats should be cooked to the correct temperatures. Check for doneness with a meat thermometer.

TURKEY MEAT LOAF

I have read that meat loaf is a traditional German dish. One quarter of Pittsburgh residents are of German descent. At one time back in history, German was actually one of the official languages of the city. From 1850 until World War II, there was a German newspaper printed in Pittsburgh.

INGREDIENTS

3 pounds ground turkey
1/2 to 1 cup plain bread crumbs
1/2 cup applesauce
1/3 cup yogurt
1 small to medium onion chopped
3 eggs
1 1/2 teaspoons salt
1/2 teaspoon black pepper

DIRECTIONS

Combine all ingredients. Form two meatloaves. Place in a foil-lined baking pan or sheet. Sprinkle top with bread crumbs or ketchup.

Bake at 350 degrees for 1 hour or until the meat thermometer reads 170 degrees.

Allow to rest for 5 minutes before cutting and serving.

PITTSBURGH EDUCATION

The Pittsburgh region is home to over sixty-eight universities and colleges as well as two major teaching hospital systems and numerous highly rated public and private preparatory schools.

The educational offerings in Pittsburgh span well beyond the offerings of formal educational institutions. There are opportunities in the city and surrounding area for those Pittsburgh residents to expand their knowledge and abilities in areas that you may not think of.

Culture and creativity go hand in hand in Pittsburgh. Glassblowing is a fascinating activity, and yes, you can take a glassblowing class in the Oakland area of the city. In 1920, Pittsburgh supplied 80 percent of all the glass in the United States. Still today, there are several small glass plants that produce their own specialty glasswork. The Oakland glassblowing center offers a variety of glass projects that change with the seasons. My favorite is the beautiful glass pumpkin that you can blow yourself during the autumn classes.

Pittsburgh has always been known for metal manufacturing. Les's Dad, Jake Niehl, worked in the copper mill, and my family worked in the steel mill. Metals are a part of Pittsburgh. If you would like to learn how to work with metals, you might like to take a blacksmith class held in the Bakery Square area. You can learn metalwork in the very important Hammer Class, where in the end you forge your own sword!

In Pittsburgh, many churches sell ethnic foods during the holidays. There is an ongoing demand for these specialties. Every year, many churches offer pierogi-making classes. It's so important to allow knowledge to filter down through generations. It is truly a gift to learn from an older experienced cook, a lesson no book can teach.

During Lent in Pittsburgh, you can take a class on making Ukrainian eggs. Pittsburgh has one of the largest populations of Ukrainians in the United States. I am a student of one such class. Over thirty years ago, I took a class for making Ukrainian eggs. I was always fascinated by the colors and curious about the technique. Since then, I have made hundreds of the time-consuming delicate eggs. I may not be Ukrainian, but I honor the philosophy and craft I was taught.

The heart of Pittsburgh is its ethnicity. Passing on the knowledge of that ethnicity is important to who we are and who we will be. Classes like these, whether they reach five or five hundred, keep our cultures alive and honor our past at the same time.

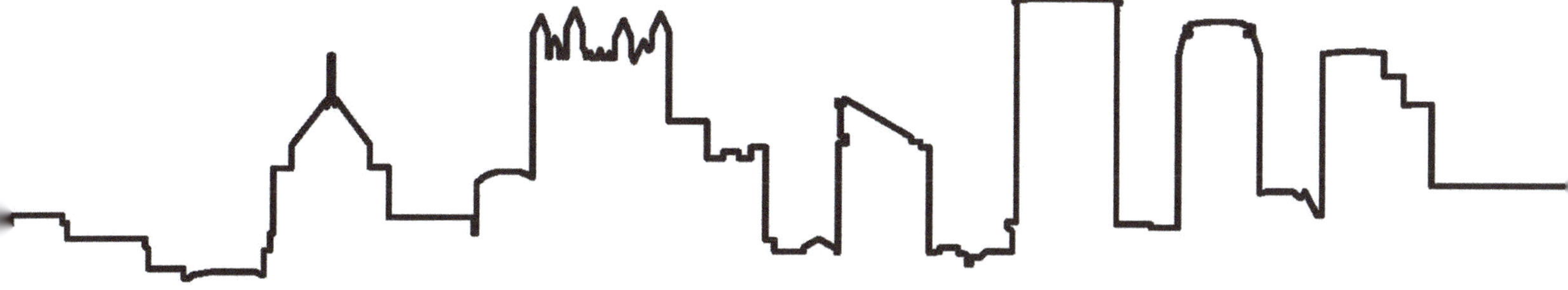

DESSERTS AND SWEETS

ANGIE'S APPLE CRISP

My mom was quite the character. She made good apple crisp. This is her recipe, which she gave to my sister-in-law, Cathy. As she got into her eighties, she was as active and independent as ever. One day, she announced at dinner that she would really appreciate it if we could buy her a new step ladder… Umm, *no*!

My favorite incident was the night she called to tell me that she could not get the basement door to lock. So she took a two-by-four and nailed the door shut. Needless to say, it was a late night for us prying, the two-by-four off and fixing the fortified door.

INGREDIENTS

1 1/2 cup flour
1 cup brown sugar
1 teaspoon cinnamon
1 cup butter plus an additional 1/4 cup butter
3 pounds of sliced, peeled apples, peaches, or blueberries
(more fruit can be added if desired)

DIRECTIONS

Mix flour, brown sugar, cinnamon, and butter together to form a crumble. Set aside half of the crumble, and place the other half on the bottom of the 13-by-9-inch glass dish. Crumble the remaining mix on top of the apples. Sprinkle with cinnamon. Dot the top layer with 1/4 cup of butter.

Bake in a 375-degree oven until apples are tender and top crust is golden.

ANGIE'S NUT ROLLS

An Italian staple made every Christmas! Cooked to a lovely chestnut brown and filled with nuts, poppy seed, or cream cheese. There is not a bakery or grocery store in Pittsburgh that does not have a variety of nut rolls in their cases. A mix between a dessert and a cookie… It doesn't get much better!

INGREDIENTS

- 8 cups flour
- 1 cup sugar
- 1 pound cold butter
- 6 eggs
- 1 cup milk
- 1 cake of yeast
- 1 1/4 cup warm water
- 1 teaspoon sugar

DIRECTIONS

With a pastry cutter or knives, cut the flour, 1 cup sugar, and the cold butter until it resembles a coarse pie dough. Set aside.

In a separate bowl, proof the yeast in the warm water with sugar.

In a separate bowl, beat the six eggs, and add the milk. Mix together with your hands the dry ingredients, the yeast mixture, and the eggs and milk.

If the dough is too sticky, add more flour if necessary. Knead the dough until your hands are clean of dough. Separate the dough into 10 pieces, and refrigerate overnight.

Roll the dough into a 13-by-9-inch piece and spread filling over it. Roll like a jelly roll, and seal the edges with water or egg. Place on a greased cookie sheet, and brush with beaten egg.

Bake at 350 degrees for 20 to 25 minutes

Nut roll fillings recipes are available on the following recipe page: "Angie's Nut Roll Fillings."

ANGIE'S NUT ROLLS FILLINGS

My Italian mom, Angie, loved to make her own fillings for her nut rolls. She didn't believe in using premade fillings. As a kid, I remember cracking the nuts and sorting the shells. Thank goodness she was eventually able to buy a bag of walnuts already shelled! Homemade filling is certainly worth the effort!

NUT FILLING

6 cups ground walnuts
1 1/2 cups brown sugar
3/4 cup butter
3/4 cup hot milk

Mix the brown sugar, butter, and milk, and add to the ground nuts.

POPPY SEED FILLING

3 jars of poppy seed
1/4 cup milk
1/2 cup sugar
4 tablespoons unsalted butter
2 ounces semisweet chocolate

Heat all ingredients together in a pan over medium to low heat. Allow to cool before using.

CREAM CHEESE FILLING

2 8-ounce packages of cream cheese, room temperature
1 cup sugar
2 eggs
1 teaspoon vanilla

Beat the cream cheese and sugar together until fluffy. Add the eggs one at a time. Add the vanilla. Beat until smooth.

ANISE BISCOTTI

Coffee ready…and dip!

INGREDIENTS

1 cup sugar
1/2 cup butter, melted
2 large eggs + 1 egg white
1 tablespoon anise extract
3 cups flour
1 tablespoon baking powder
1/2 teaspoon salt
1 tablespoon milk + 1 egg yolk

DIRECTIONS

Cream butter and sugar until fluffy. Beat in the 2 large eggs, egg white, and the anise extract.

In a separate bowl, mix the flour, baking powder, and salt together with a wooden spoon. Stir together the butter mix and the flour mix.

On a floured board, knead the mix for 1–2 minutes until the dough is smooth. Divide the dough in half, and shape each into a long log—3 inches wide and 10 inches long.

Beat the reserved egg yolk and milk, and brush the loaf before baking.

Bake in a 375-degree oven until golden brown, about 15 to 20 minutes.

When cooled, slice each loaf into 1-inch slices. Place slices on a cookie sheet, and put them under the broiler. Allow them to toast briefly until brown on the edges.

This biscotti can be made using vanilla or almond extract in place of the anise.

BOURBON BANANA CAKE

Not your mother's banana cake, but who said that was a bad thing!

INGREDIENTS

1/2 cup salted butter
1 1/2 cup sugar
4 eggs
4 ripe bananas, sliced
1 cup sour cream
1 teaspoon baking soda
1 teaspoon salt
21/2 cups all-purpose flour
1/4 cup bourbon
1 teaspoon vanilla

DIRECTIONS

In a bowl, mix together the dry ingredients, and set aside.

Using a mixer, cream together the butter and sugar until the mix is light and fluffy. Add the eggs one at a time, and continue to beat on medium speed. Beat in the sliced ripe bananas and sour cream. Add the dry ingredients to the banana mix. Finally, add the bourbon and vanilla, and mix on medium speed until fully incorporated.

Pour the cake mixture into a well-greased fluted pan or bundt pan.

Bake at 350 degrees for 60 to 65 minutes. Test with a cake tester to make sure it is fully cooked. Allow to cool in the fluted pan for 10 minutes before transferring to a serving dish.

This cake can be dusted with powdered sugar or drizzled with a brown sugar caramel icing.

BROWN SUGAR WHIPPED CREAM

A great topping for so many fall apple desserts! Pittsburgh is home to many apple festivals. Pennsylvania ranks fourth in the nation in production of apples. Each year, 400 to 500 million pounds are grown. This delicious whipped cream is great with apple or pumpkin pie, apple crisp, or even a baked apple.

INGREDIENTS

2 cups heavy cream
1/4 cup light brown sugar

DIRECTIONS

Whip the heavy cream until soft peaks form. Add in the brown sugar, and continue to whip. Store the leftover whipped cream in a colander placed in a bowl in the refrigerator.

CHEREGI

This is my grandma Mary's recipe for what she called Wandees. Grandma was very Italian. At one time, she worked in the pickle factory during the day and was a "bookie" on the side. Her brothers took her numbers bets in the mills where they worked. She had a gravelly voice, a mole to the side of her lip, and always had a cigarette. She gave my brother and me a dollar every time she would leave to go home. Every Christmas morning, she faithfully made the Wandees for us all to enjoy!

Wait. Isn't everybody's grandma the same?

INGREDIENTS

1 tablespoon sugar
1 egg
1 tablespoon heavy cream
1/4 teaspoon salt
1/2 teaspoon vanilla
3/4 cup flour

DIRECTIONS

Beat egg until very fluffy. Add sugar, cream, salt, and vanilla. Mix in the flour to make a dough.

Roll the dough on a lightly floured board until very thin. Cut into 3-inch squares. Cut a slit in the center of each square. Thread one corner through the hole and pull.

Fry in hot oil, and sprinkle with powdered sugar.

CHOCOLATE BUTTERCREAM FROSTING

This is a light and fluffy topping for the best of cakes! Pittsburgh has had numerous family bakeries, many of them known for specialty items that they made so well. Some had unique cakes, breads, or cookies that were usually old ethnic recipes that their ancestors brought with them when they immigrated to Pittsburgh. Seemed like every little town had a family bakery.

INGREDIENTS

3/4 cup softened butter
1/4 cup shortening
1/2 cup unsweetened cocoa
dash of salt
1 tablespoon vanilla
51/2 cups powdered sugar
1/2 cup heavy cream

DIRECTIONS

Cream together the butter and shortening until smooth. Add the salt and cocoa, and continue to beat. Add the vanilla. Add the powdered sugar and heavy cream alternatively, and continue to beat. Scrape the sides of the bowl throughout the process. Beat until the frosting is fluffy.

CHOCOLATE COFFEE FUDGE

My mom, Angie, loved fudge. Every trip to Kennywood Amusement Park in the West Mifflin section of Pittsburgh always ended with a stop at the Fudge Shop. It was and is the best!

INGREDIENTS

1 3/4 cups pecans, toasted and chopped
41/2 cups semisweet chocolate morsels
1 1/2 cans sweetened condensed milk
1/4 cup strongly brewed coffee, room temperature
1/4 teaspoon salt
2 teaspoons vanilla

DIRECTIONS

Line an 8-by-8-inch pan with foil, and butter the foil. Set aside for later use.

In a skillet, place pecans, and heat on medium heat to allow the nuts to roast. Carefully toss over the heat, allowing to slightly brown but not burn. Set aside.

In a double boiler, heat chocolate morsels until melted, and add the sweetened condensed milk. Mix well, and stir in the coffee. Next, add the pecans, and follow with the salt and vanilla.

Completely mix, and immediately spread into the prepared pan. Cover, and refrigerate for 3 hours.

Once set, remove fudge from pan, and cut into 1-inch squares. Store in an airtight container at room temperature.

CONCESSION STAND GIANT COOKIES

I put this recipe together so we could offer a sweet treat for the kids at the Penn-Trafford football games. Les and I operated two concession stands for eight years, and we loved every minute! These cookies are so large that only six cookies fit on a standard cookie sheet. They are a great mix of flavors!

INGREDIENTS

- 1 cup unsalted butter, softened
- 1 cup shortening
- 2 cups sugar
- 2 cups brown sugar
- 4 large eggs
- 1 tablespoon vanilla
- 4 cups flour
- 2 teaspoons baking powder
- 2 teaspoons baking soda
- 1 12-ounce bag of chocolate chips
- 1 teaspoon salt
- 2 cups quick oats
- 2 cups corn flakes
- 1 cup coconut
- 1 cup walnuts

DIRECTIONS

Cream together the butter and shortening, and add in the sugars. Beat until fluffy. Add the eggs one at a time, and then the vanilla.

Sift together the flour, salt, baking soda, and powder, and beat into the creamed sugar mix. Stir in the remaining ingredients.

Using an ice cream scoop, drop cookies on a lightly greased cookie sheet.

This makes about 12–15 cookies.

Bake in a 350-degree oven for 20 minutes or until golden.

EASY NUT FUDGE

This is a very easy way to make fudge. The most complicated part is the double boiler! Pittsburgh is known for its "complicated" Fort Pitt Bridge coming into the city. It provides an amazing burst of the city scene. Most Pittsburghers are proud to drive guests from the airport into the city to enjoy this view. However, just below are the four lanes going into the tunnel heading away from town. It is a navigational nightmare—four lanes of traffic doing an extreme merge. Some drivers have a mere three hundred feet to go from the extreme right lane to the extreme left lane—all this accomplished on a bridge above the Monongahela River. Three hundred feet of traffic mayhem! Just makes you shake your head. It's so Pittsburgh!

INGREDIENTS

1 pound confectioners' sugar
1/2 cup cocoa
1/4 teaspoon salt
3 ounces butter
1/4 cup whole milk
1 tablespoon vanilla
1 cup pecans, toasted and chopped

DIRECTIONS

Mix together the sugar, cocoa, and salt, and set aside.

In a double boiler, allow the butter to melt, and add the rest of the wet and dry ingredients. Stir with a wooden spoon until all the ingredients are well mixed. Remove from the heat, and stir in the nuts.

Spread in an 8-by-8-inch buttered foil-lined pan.

Cool for 2 hours, and refrigerate.

CRISSCROSS PASTRY

My husband Les's family has spent summers at Lake Pymatuning, Pennsylvania, for over fifty years. They are a talented, resourceful, and very fun bunch. This dessert is one of their favorites. They affectionately call it Cherries Espyville, named after the small village on the lake. Many evenings at that wonderful cottage were spent enjoying this dessert!

INGREDIENTS

2 1/4 cups sugar
3/4 cup shortening
3/4 cup butter
2 1/4 baking powder
1/2 teaspoon salt
2 teaspoons vanilla
6 eggs
4 1/2 cups flour
3 cans pie filling

DIRECTIONS

Beat together the sugar, butter, and shortening until fluffy. Add the eggs one at a time and then the vanilla.

In a separate bowl, sift together the flour, baking powder, and salt. Beat into the sugar-and-buttercream mix.

Spread 2/3 of the batter onto a greased cookie sheet. Carefully spread the pie filling on top of the spread batter.

Using a decorator bag, pipe the remaining dough in a crisscross pattern over the pie filling.

Bake at 350 degrees for 45 minutes or until golden.

Cool and serve.

FRUIT PASTRY TART

This tart comes alive with the fresh fruit of summer. Such a beautiful presentation! The crust should be flaky pastry and not a store-bought tube of cookie dough.

INGREDIENTS

For the crust:

- 1 cup flour
- 1/4 teaspoon salt
- 1/4 cup sugar
- 1/2 cup chilled unsalted butter cut into pieces
- 4 1/2 ounces soft cream cheese

For the filling:

- 8 ounces soft cream cheese
- 1/2 cup sugar
- 1 teaspoon vanilla

For the glaze:

- 1 jar of apricot jam

DIRECTIONS

To make the tart, combine dry ingredients in a bowl. Cut in butter and cream cheese with a pastry blender until it forms a coarse crumble.

Form into a ball, and cover and refrigerate overnight.

Press into tart pan. Bake at 450 degrees for 10–12 minutes.

The tart recipe can be doubled if needed.

For the filling, mix together the ingredients for the filling, and spread the mixture over the baked crust. Cut a variety of fruit in slices, and arrange them on the tart (strawberries, kiwi, blueberries, grapes, raspberries, etc.).

To make the glaze, heat the apricot jam until it is very fluid, and using a pastry brush, coat the entire pie with the glaze. It adds flavor, seals the fruit, and give a nice finished look.

Chill and serve.

GIANT GINGER COOKIES

These cookies are so scrumptious, and as an extra bonus, they make your house smell like Christmas! Great with coffee, tea, and milk! I understand Santa loves these cookies as well!

INGREDIENTS

4 1/2 cups all-purpose flour
1 tablespoon + 1 teaspoon ginger
2 teaspoons baking soda
1 1/2 teaspoons ground cinnamon
1/2 teaspoon ground clove
1/2 cup molasses
1/2 teaspoon salt
1 1/2 cups butter, softened
2 cups granulated sugar
2 eggs
2 tablespoon water
coarse sugar to coat

DIRECTIONS

Sift together the flour, baking soda, ginger, cinnamon, clove, and salt. Set this aside.

In a large bowl, cream together the butter and sugar until fluffy. Beat in the eggs, then the molasses and water. Beat until well blended. Slowly beat in the sifted dry ingredients.

Using a large 2-inch cookie scoop, make balls, and roll each in the coarse sugar.

Bake in a 350-degree oven. Place 6 cookies on the cookie sheet at a time. Bake the cookies for 18 minutes or until done. Allow to cool on the cookie sheet before removing.

Store in an airtight container.

HOMEMADE FRUIT PIE FILLING

Honestly, try this. It is like magic. Let it cook long enough for the cornstarch to work. One second, it is a liquid, and the next, it is like a can of pie filling.

INGREDIENTS

4–6 cups fresh fruit (cherries, blueberries, etc.)
1 cup granulated white sugar
1/3 cup cornstarch
1 tablespoon butter

DIRECTIONS

Clean, rinse, and drain the fruit. Place in a large heavy saucepot and place over low/medium heat. Stirring often, allow the fruit to release juices.

In a separate bowl, whisk together the sugar and cornstarch. When the fruit is heated through, add the sugar-and-cornstarch mix, and incorporate through the fruit. Add the butter. Cook and stir over medium heat.

As the fruit cooks, it will thicken. When the filling is to pie consistency, remove from the heat. Once the filling is warm to the touch, it can be placed in prepared pie crust and baked.

GRANDMA LUTTON'S FAMOUS SUNSHINE CAKE

Anna Mae McCall Lutton was my grandma, and she was known for this special cake. Grandma had stunning white hair, and she enjoyed bowling, playing pinochle, and doing her amazing needlepoint. We spent many summers with her and my Grandpap Howard at their cottage in Conneaut Lake, Pennsylvania.

INGREDIENTS

5 egg yolks
1/2 cup sugar
1 cup sifted cake flour
2 tablespoon cold water
1 teaspoon vanilla
1/2 teaspoon lemon extract
1/2 teaspoon orange extract

8 egg whites
1/2 teaspoon cream of tarter
1/2 teaspoon salt
1 cup sugar

DIRECTIONS

Beat 1/2 cup sugar into the egg yolks. In a separate bowl, combine the flour, salt, and cream of tarter, and set aside.

In a clean metal mixing bowl, beat the egg whites to soft peaks. Gradually add the 1 cup of sugar, and continue to beat until it forms stiff peaks. Set this aside.

Add the vanilla, orange, and lemon extract into the egg yolk mixture. Add the flour mixture into the egg yolks. Once completely mixed, fold the beaten egg whites into the flour / egg yolk mixture. Carefully fold until the two mixtures are fully incorporated before placing into the baking pan.

Grease an angel food/tube pan or a 13-by-9-inch pan.

Bake in a 325-degree oven for 60–65 minutes or until it tests done.

Ice with an orange drizzle or orange buttercream.

ITALIAN CRÈME CAKE

This cake will make you want to eat dessert first!

INGREDIENTS

For the cake:

- 1 1/2 cups sugar
- 1/2 cup butter
- 1/2 cup shortening
- 5 large eggs, separated
- 2 cups flour
- 1 cup buttermilk, with 1 teaspoon baking soda added
- 1 cup coconut

For the frosting:

- 12 ounces cream cheese
- 3/4 cup butter
- 1 1/2 pounds confectioners' sugar
- 2 teaspoons almond flavoring
- 3/4 cup ground walnuts

DIRECTIONS

Cream the sugar, butter, and shortening together. Add the egg yolks one at a time, and beat well. Alternatively, beat in the flour and buttermilk mix. Beat well. Stir in the coconut. In separate bowl, beat the egg whites until stiff, and fold into batter.

Bake in 4 greased and floured pans at 350 degrees for 20–25 minutes or until an inserted toothpick comes out clean. Allow cakes to cool.

Beat the cream cheese and butter. When beaten well, add the confectioners' sugar and almond extract and beat until fluffy.

Frost cake. The ground walnuts can be used between layers and on top or can be added into the frosting.

LEMON FUDGE

My mom, Angie Cerrone Lutton, loved her fudge. This is one of her many recipes. It is refreshing! My mother used to make this fudge for my grandmother who lived in Braddock. On Sundays, when we would pick Grandma up to go to dinner "down the house," she often put a chair in the street next to the curb in front of her house to save us a parking place. This is known as the famous Pittsburgh "chair." You see Pittsburgh chairs all over town, saving parking places. Strangely enough, this unwritten law in Pittsburgh is widely respected. Nobody moves a Pittsburgh chair.

INGREDIENTS

6 tablespoons butter
20–24 ounces white chocolate chips
2/3 cup sweetened condensed milk
2/3 cup marshmallow cream
2 teaspoons lemon extract

DIRECTIONS

Line an 8-by-8-inch pan with foil, and grease with butter. Set this aside.

In a heavy saucepan, melt the butter using low heat to ensure the butter does not burn. Add the white chocolate chips and sweetened condensed milk. Cook and stir this mix for 10–12 minutes using a wooden spoon. Make sure the chips are completely melted.

Stir in the marshmallow cream and the lemon extract. When the mix is totally incorporated, pour into the prepared pan, and chill.

To serve, lift the foil out of the pan, and cut into squares. Store in the refrigerator.

Yield: 2 pounds.

LOIS ROBINSON'S TOFFEE BARS

The Robinson family lived two houses from ours. They were the first Swedish family I have ever met. Being Italian and Irish, I had never seen such blond hair! They were all very beautiful. I remember they called their couch a davenport. They were so welcoming, gracious, and kind. There are quite a few Swedes in Pittsburgh. Each year, they have an annual food celebration during the holiday season.

INGREDIENTS

1 cup brown sugar
1/2 cup butter, softened
1/2 cup shortening
1 egg yolk
2 cups flour
1/8 teaspoon salt
1/2 cup nuts (optional)
1 cup toffee chips
1 cup chocolate chips, melted

DIRECTIONS

Cream together the butter and shortening until smooth. Beat in egg yolk. Once incorporated, blend in flour and salt. Stir in toffee chips.

Lightly grease a cookie sheet. Spread the batter into the pan evenly.

Bake at 350 degrees for 20 minutes or until an inserted toothpick comes out clean.

Remove from oven, and immediately ice with melted chocolate.

MADDIE'S MAGICAL BROWN SUGAR COOKIES

Cookies from the heart and imagination of a six-year-old! Maddie is my brother Tom's granddaughter. Les and I have been blessed to babysit her since she was born. She has been raised cooking with me, so it did not surprise me when she wanted to make her own cookies.

INGREDIENTS

1 stick salted butter, softened
1 cup brown sugar
2 cups flour
2 eggs
1/4 cup whole milk or cream

DIRECTIONS

Cream together the butter and brown sugar until smooth. Beat in the eggs, adding one at a time. Continue to beat until the mix is very fluffy and light. Gradually add alternating amounts of the flour and milk. If batter is too stiff, you can add a bit more milk.

Use a cookie scoop, and place each piece on a greased cookie sheet.

Bake in a 350 degree oven for 15 minutes or until done.

MASHED POTATO FUDGE

Many Irish immigrants came to Pittsburgh during the potato famine. My ancestors came to Western Pennsylvania in 1750 before the famine hit Ireland. Pittsburgh is 14 percent Irish and is home to many chapters of the Ancient Order of Hibernians and Lady Hibernians. Pittsburgh is certainly Irish proud, and they have one of the largest Saint Patrick's Day parades in the nation. In 2019, there were twenty-three thousand participants in the parade with two hundred marching units, floats, and a leprechaun or two!

INGREDIENTS

3 ounces unsweetened chocolate
1 tablespoon butter
1/2 teaspoon vanilla
1/4 cup mashed potato
2 cups sifted confectioners' sugar

DIRECTIONS

Place chocolate and butter in a double boiler, and allow to melt. Once fully melted, add the potato and vanilla. Gradually add the confectioners' sugar, stirring with a wooden spoon.

Once you can no longer stir any more, sugar into the mix, place the mix on to a board, and knead in the remaining sugar. Once the sugar is fully incorporated, press fudge into an 8-by-8-inch pan.

Store fudge in airtight container or covered pan. Can be kept in the refrigerator for 2 weeks.

MY FAVORITE NIECE'S PEANUT BRITTLE (KIM POTTER)

Kim is an amazing artist with such a great wit. There is nothing she can't build or fix! She loves an afternoon in her kayak on Lake Pymatuning with a good book and a tall glass of iced tea.

INGREDIENTS

1 1/2 cups sugar
1 cup corn syrup
1 cup water
1 pound nuts
candy thermometer

1 1/2 teaspoon baking soda
1 teaspoon water
1 teaspoon vanilla
3 tablespoon butter

DIRECTIONS

Mix the baking soda, teaspoon of water, and vanilla, and set aside.

In a heavy saucepan, cook the sugar, corn syrup, and one cup of water until it reaches 240 degrees on a candy thermometer. Stirring often, continue to cook until the mix reaches 300 degrees. At 300 degrees, add the nuts and butter, and allow the mix to return to 300 degrees. Continue to stir. When the mix reaches 300 degrees, turn off the heat, and add the baking soda mixture. Stir vigorously to incorporate.

Pour on to a lightly buttered cookie sheet and spread. Allow to cool for 1 hour, and break into pieces.

Store in an airtight container. This recipe can be doubled.

MY FAVORITE NIECE'S PEANUT BUTTER BROWNIES (GINNY KUKLEWSKI)

Ginny is such a genuine person. She is down-to-earth, and if you want to have fun, make sure she is on the guest list. We have often joked about being in-laws together. She's fun to play Scrabble with as long as you don't look at her letters!

INGREDIENTS

For the batter:

- 1/2 cup unsalted butter, softened
- 1 cup sugar
- 16 ounces chocolate syrup
- 4 eggs
- 1 cup flour

For the topping:

- 1 cup peanut butter
- 8 ounces milk chocolate
- 1 teaspoon oil

DIRECTIONS

Combine all the batter ingredients. Mix by hand until the batter is formed. Pour into a lightly greased 13-by-9-inch dish.

Bake for 30 minutes in a 350-degree oven.

While hot, spread the peanut butter over the cooked brownie, then chill. Melt the chocolate and oil together, and spread over the chilled peanut butter. Chill until the chocolate has hardened.

NO-BAKE COOKIES

If there was a neighborhood cookie on Dunbar Drive, it was these no-bake cookies. Bobbi Willis was known for them. She would mix them up and, using a wooden spoon, with some force, thwack them right onto the wax paper-covered counter. Mary Jane Willis Schultz, Harry Willis, Bonnie Pearson Miller, Linda Robinson Payne, Greg Robinson, and Jimmy Harvey! No words were ever said. We all were just drawn to the counter for that amazing warm goodness.

INGREDIENTS

2 cups sugar
1/2 cup unsalted butter
3 tablespoons cocoa
1/2 cup milk
3/4 cup peanut butter
1 teaspoon vanilla
3 cups oatmeal

DIRECTIONS

Mix the sugar, cocoa, and milk in a heavy saucepan. Add the butter, and cook over medium heat. Bring to a full rolling boil, and allow to boil for 1 1/2 minutes. Remove from the heat, and add the peanut butter, vanilla, and oatmeal. Mix thoroughly. Drop by teaspoons (unless you want to use the Bobbi Willis "thwacking" method!) on to wax paper, and allow to cool and firm. Call the kids—or just open a window! Make these cookies, and the kids will come!

PEANUT BUTTER FUDGE

This fudge works best with a cold glass of milk! Pittsburgh and the Western Pennsylvania area are home to many dairy farms. There are nine dairies that offer their own delicious ice cream. Many Pittsburghers take the "dairy trail" to taste each dairy's sweet contribution!

INGREDIENTS

1 cup butter
1 cup peanut butter
1/4 cup cocoa
2 tablespoons vanilla extract
1 pound confectioners' sugar

DIRECTIONS

Line an 8-by-8-inch pan with foil, and butter it. Set this aside.

In a heavy saucepan, melt the butter and peanut butter together. When completely melted and combined, add the vanilla extract. Remove from heat, and beat in the confections' sugar.

Pour the fudge into the prepared pan, and allow to cool.

PUMPKIN FUDGE

My dear friend Jill Hess introduced me to this fudge. You might be hesitant to put pumpkin into a fudge recipe, but trust me—it works! Take your time, and allow the mixture to cook to the soft ball stage. The result will be a rich creamy fudge that is a real autumn treat.

INGREDIENTS

- 3 cups sugar
- 3/4 cup melted butter
- 2/3 cup evaporated milk
- 1/2 cup canned pumpkin puree
- 2 tablespoons corn syrup
- 1 teaspoon pumpkin pie spice
- 12-ounce bag white chocolate chips
- cooking/candy thermometer (recommended)
- 7-ounce marshmallow cream
- 1 teaspoon vanilla extract
- 1 cup chopped nuts, optional

DIRECTIONS

Line a 9-by-13-inch dish with foil, and spray with cooking spray.

Stir together the sugar, melted butter, evaporated milk, pumpkin, corn syrup, and the pumpkin pie spice in a large heavy saucepan. With candy thermometer attached to the side of your saucepan, heat over medium heat, stirring constantly until the mixture reaches the soft ball stage or 234 degrees on the thermometer. Remove from heat, and quickly add in the white chocolate chips, marshmallow, vanilla, and chopped nuts (if you choose to use them). Stir until all ingredients are incorporated.

Pour into the prepared pan, and allow to set for 2 hours or until completely cooled. This makes 3 pounds of fudge.

PUMPKIN PIE CAKE

This recipe is the best of two worlds—cake on the bottom and pie on the top!

INGREDIENTS

For the crust:

1 box yellow cake plus mix
1/2 cup butter, melted
1 egg, beaten

For the filling:

1 large can pumpkin puree
1 teaspoon cinnamon or pumpkin pie spice
2/3 cup evaporated milk
3 eggs, beaten
1 1/4 cups white granulated sugar
1/2 brown sugar
2/3 cup walnuts, chopped and toasted (optional for the topping)

DIRECTIONS

Combine the cake mix, butter, and egg with a fork until the mix resembles crumbs. Set aside 1 cup of the crumbs. The rest of the crumbs should be pressed into a greased and floured 13-by-9-inch pan.

In a separate bowl, mix the pumpkin, cinnamon or pumpkin pie spice, evaporated milk, eggs, and sugars. Pour into the crust, and top with the remaining crumbles. A sprinkle of white granulated sugar can be added on top of the crumbles.

Bake in a 350-degree oven for 50 to 55 minutes until a knife inserted is clean when removed.

Serve with whipped cream.

SNOW-WHITE FRUITED FUDGE

This is one of the many fudge recipes from my mom, Angie. She loved fruit-and-nut eggs at Easter. This fudge is similar to the fondant filling in those eggs. It is a nice change of pace flavor!

INGREDIENTS

2 pounds white chocolate melting disks
1 cup whipping cream
1/4 teaspoon salt
1/2 cup chopped candied cherries (red or green)
1/3 cup chopped candied pineapple

DIRECTIONS

Place the white chocolate disks in a double boiler. Simmer and stir the disks, allowing them to melt. Remove the white chocolate from the heat, and set aside.

In a small saucepot, heat the whipping cream and salt on low heat. Stir the mixture with a wooden spoon, and using a candy thermometer, allow mix to reach 160 degrees.

Pour the whipping cream and salt into the melted white chocolate. Blend in the candied fruit.

Pour into a buttered 8-by-8-inch pan, and allow to set.

SOUR CREAM NUT ROLLS

Our Pittsburgh Slovaks make great nut rolls. No other city in the United States has more people of Slovak descent than Pittsburgh. In the late 1800s, over 100,000 Slovakian immigrants arrived in Pittsburgh to find work and make a new life.

INGREDIENTS

1/2 cake household yeast—1/3 cup warm water with 1/2 teaspoon sugar
1/2 cup butter
3 tablespoon butter
1/2 cup sour cream
31/2 cups flour
filling of your choice

DIRECTIONS

Proof the yeast in the warm water and sugar, and set aside. Cream the butter and sugar. Add one egg at a time, and beat until smooth. Beat in the sour cream and the yeast mixture. Stir the flour in by hand, and knead until a smooth dough is formed.

Divide the dough into 3 or 4 pieces, and cover until ready to fill. Roll dough into a 13-by-9-inch piece, not too thin. Spread desired filling, roll like a jelly roll, and seal the ends.

Place on a well-greased cookie sheet, and cover with a towel. Allow to rise for 1 hour. Prick the top of the nut rolls before baking.

Bake at 350 degrees for 30 to 35 minutes.

SOUR CREAM PASTRY

This is a versatile recipe for tarts or pastries. It pairs well with fruit or cream and complements custard.

INGREDIENTS

2 cups all-purpose flour, sifted
1/2 teaspoon salt
1/4 cup sour cream
filling and/or topping of your choice
1/2 teaspoon baking powder
1/2 cup shortening
1 egg, beaten

DIRECTIONS

Place flour, salt, and baking powder in a bowl. Using a pastry blender, cut the shortening in until the mixture is coarse. Mix in the sour cream and egg until the you can form the mixture into a ball.

Chill at least for 1 hour before using. This can be blind-baked if needed.

SPHINGI (SFINGI)

These bites are Italian doughnuts! This recipe is my great-grandmother's. Many nationalities make their own doughnuts. I make doughnuts each year on Fat Tuesday—on the eve of Lent. We and our neighbors eat like fools with no regret!

INGREDIENTS

2 cups ricotta
1 1/2 cups flour (more if needed)
6 teaspoons baking powder
4 eggs
1 teaspoon vanilla
frying oil

DIRECTIONS

With an electric mixer, beat the ricotta until smooth and fluffy. Add the eggs one at a time, and beat well.

In a small bowl, mix together the flour and baking powder. Add the dry ingredients and the vanilla to the ricotta mixture, and mix well. Allow this to stand for 30 minutes. The mixture will fluff up. If at this point, the mixture seems too thin, add a small amount of flour to thicken so it resembles a thick batter.

Heat oil to 375 degrees. Drop teaspoons of batter into the hot oil, and fry until golden brown. Remove with slotted spoon, and drain on a paper towel. Sprinkle with powdered sugar and serve.

Yield: 3 or 4 dozen.

STRUFFOLI

One Christmas, I made this for my mom as a surprise. She had talked about her grandmother making it for her as a little girl. Mom grew up in the family house since my grandfather died when she was only two years old. My grandmother was only nineteen years old and a widow. Sometimes the paths we travel are not easy. This was a very meaningful Christmas gift to her, and I was thrilled to make it happen.

INGREDIENTS

6 cups flour
pinch of salt
12 eggs
1 cup sugar
3 tablespoons (heaping) shortening
3 tablespoons oil
4 teaspoons baking powder
1 teaspoon lemon extract
1 1/4 cup honey
multicolored nonpareils

DIRECTIONS

Combine all the ingredients except the honey and 1/2 cup of the sugar. Mix to a batter, and fry either strips or balls of dough in hot oil. When golden brown, remove, and drain on paper towels. Place on a serving dish. Mix the honey and sugar together, and drizzle over the fried dough. Sprinkle with decorator sugar nonpareils.

SUMMER PEACH CAKE

I went to Churchill Area High School. I had a group of friends that were, to say the least, a hoot! We had fun every way we could. One of our events was a progressive dinner. The seven of us were Melanie Kneip-Davison, Jill Gonella-Tubbs, Karen Sotak-Dear, Jan McMahon, Dr. Jeanne DeMoss, and Nina Patterson-Hansen, and myself. We enjoyed a different course at each other's house, and it literally took all night. My course was dessert that night—this cake! I miss those girls and the many escapades, the simple lives we led, and of course, the laughs we had.

INGREDIENTS

29-ounce can sliced peaches, drained (reserving liquid)
1 package super moist yellow cake mix
3 eggs
1 1/4 cup reserved peach liquid (add water if needed)
1/3 cup oil
6-ounce container peach yogurt
8-ounce container frozen whipped topping

DIRECTIONS

Heat oven to 350 degrees. Grease and flour two 9-inch cake pans. Beat together the cake mix, eggs, oil, and peach liquid. Beat for 2 minutes. Divide into the cake pans, and bake for 25 to 30 minutes or until an inserted toothpick comes out clean. Cool completely.

Mix the whipped topping and yogurt. Spread the topping-and-yogurt mixture between the layers and on the top of the cake. Chopped peaches can be placed along with the topping-and-yogurt mixture between the layers of the cake. Do not spread this mixture on the sides of the cake. Use the peach slices to decorate—either by chopping them or using them whole.

Chill for 2 hours before serving.

TORTE PASTRY

This is a useful recipe to keep in your book, just in case! Tortes are great desserts. They can be filled with many different fillings. This is an old recipe which I would think you could mix using a dough hook on your stand mixer.

INGREDIENTS

1/2 cup unsalted butter
1 2/3 cup all-purpose flour, sifted
1 1/2 teaspoon baking powder
2 tablespoons sugar
1/2 teaspoon salt
2 egg yolks

DIRECTIONS

Place the dry ingredients in a bowl. Using a pastry blender, cut the butter into the mix. Add the egg yolks, and knead the mixture into a ball. The dough can then be patted into a pan.

Sweet dough can be made by increasing the flour to 1 3/4 cups and increasing the sugar to 1/3 cup. Omit the salt, and proceed as above.

PITTSBURGH COOKIE TABLES

Pittsburgh has a very unique tradition. Pittsburghers are known for their cookie tables at weddings. This tradition began during the Great Depression (1930s) when many Italian, Polish, and other ethnic families did not have enough money to include a wedding cake at their weddings. The mother of the bride assumed the responsibility of providing the wedding meal for her guests. In an effort to provide a dessert, the mother of the bride would bake cookies in place of the cake. She was joined with her family in her efforts. Grandmothers, aunts, sisters, and cousins—all baked cookies to help with the wedding.

The tradition has never stopped. In fact, it has grown! Wedding cookie displays are a very serious matter. The selection of cookies offered as well as the number of cookies is a coordinated effort. The rule of thumb is that a table should provide six to twelve cookies per guest. The variety of cookies is also a very important decision. There are types of cookies that Pittsburghers expect to find on their cookie table. First and foremost would be lady locks, pizzelles, cookies resembling peaches, la dolche (Italian wedding cookies), kolacky, thumbprints, pignoli, and miniature cheesecake cookies. The person coordinating the cookie table always tries to make sure there is true variety and ample supply.

Cookies are often plated, and the table is decorated to the theme of the wedding (e.g., rustic). It is important to visualize the textures and colors of the cookies as well as the lighting, décor, and varied heights of the plating. I have also seen weddings where a table was covered with white paper and the cookies were arranged in a mosaic pattern in swirls of goodness and colors of icings, nuts, and textures. It takes a keen eye and artistic hand to arrange such tables.

Cookies are usually served with the cake. Cookie tables are covered in some manner until after dinner. There is usually some little old studda bubba grandma who raids the covered table before dinner. Most people understand and abide by the unwritten rules. Along with the small serving plates for guests to gather their choices, there often are containers for guests to take cookies home as well.

We in Pittsburgh are so proud of our cookie tables. I think what is most impressive to me is the outpouring of help with each wedding. Many times I have told friends and family that I would be happy to help with the cookies, whether I am invited to the wedding or not. It is just the neighborly Pittsburgh family thing to do.

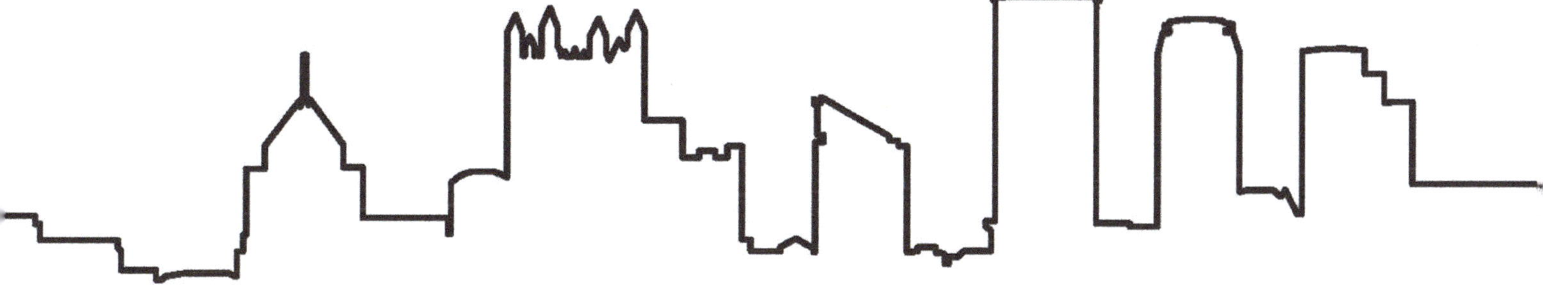

PITTSBURGH COOKIE TABLE COOKIES

ALMOND CRESCENTS

These cookies provide a different shape to the cookie table. It's important to vary the shapes, sizes, textures, and colors on the table. Remember, if a cookie looks good to your eyes, it usually tastes better in your mouth. If possible, the cookie trays should also be placed at various levels, which allows accents like lighting, flowers, floral greens, and specialty candies or confections to be added.

INGREDIENTS

1 cup unsalted butter, softened
3/4 cup confectioners' sugar, sifted
1/4 teaspoon salt
1 teaspoon vanilla extract
1/4 teaspoon almond extract
3/4 cup almonds, ground
21/4 cups sifted flour

DIRECTIONS

Cream together the butter and confectioners' sugar until smooth. Add in the remaining ingredients, and beat until a dough forms. Dough may be stiff, and kneading may help to ensure that all the ingredients are incorporated. Roll dough into pencil thick logs, and cut into a length of 2 1/4 inches. Form crescents of each length, and place on a greased cookie sheet.

Bake in a 325-degree oven for 18–20 minutes. Cookies should not be allowed to brown; rather they should be baked until pale but baked through.

When cookies are still warm, roll in confectioners' sugar.

ANGIE LUTTON'S SOUR CREAM COOKIES

These were my mother's favorite. When she made cookies, she made these! I would come home to find the entire dining room table filled to the edge with sour cream cookies. What a great memory! My dad loved them with his coffee.

INGREDIENTS

For the cookies:

- 1/2 cup unsalted butter
- 1 1/2 cups sugar
- 2 large eggs
- 1 cup sour cream
- 1 teaspoon vanilla
- 2 3/4 cups sifted flour
- 1/2 teaspoon baking powder
- 1/2 teaspoon baking soda
- 1/2 salt

For the icing:

- 4 tablespoons unsalted butter
- 1 cup sifted confectioner's sugar
- 1/2 teaspoon vanilla
- 1–2 tablespoons hot water

DIRECTIONS

Beat the butter and sugar. Once fully mixed, add the eggs one at a time. Continue beating until fluffy. Beat in the sour cream and vanilla. Sift together the flour, baking powder, baking soda, and salt, and gradually beat into the egg mixture. Chill for several hours or overnight.

Drop rounded teaspoons on to lightly greased cookie sheets.

Bake in a 425-degree oven for 8–10 minutes.

Cool and frost. Yield: 5 dozen.

For the icing, melt butter until golden. Blend in confectioners' sugar and vanilla. Stir in hot water until the icing is smooth and spreadable. Ice cookies, and allow to dry before storing between waxed paper sheets.

CAKE FLOUR PIZZELLES

Pittsburgh families work very hard to make sure the cookies at a wedding are a beautiful presentation. Pizzelles are always offered. These are a very light and crispy cookie made on a waffle-like hinged grill called a pizzelle iron. Pizzelle irons are popular shower gifts for future brides. Now you can even order an iron that bakes the surname initial in the center of each cookie!

INGREDIENTS

1 pound unsalted butter, melted
31/4 cup sugar
9 jumbo eggs
4 cups flour
1 cup cake flour
1 teaspoon baking powder
1 tablespoon vanilla extract
1/4 cup whiskey

DIRECTIONS

Sift together the flours and baking powder, and set aside. Using a mixer, beat together the eggs and sugar. Allow the melted butter to cool slightly so as not to cook the eggs. Add the cooled melted butter to the eggs. When completely mixed, add the vanilla, anise, and whiskey. Gradually beat in the sifted flours and baking powder until the batter has been formed.

Spoon the batter onto a lightly greased hot pizzelle iron. Close the iron, and bake until golden brown.

CARAMEL CUPS

Boy, these are so tasty. The buttery caramel and soothing smooth filling just screams, "I am a dessert!" But the cookie cup says, "Nope, just an awesome cookie!" These are a great addition to any cookie table!

INGREDIENTS

For the dough:
- 6 ounces cream cheese, softened
- 3/4 cup unsalted butter
- 2 cups flour

For the filling:
- 1 11-ounce bag of caramels
- 1/2 cup evaporated milk
- 1/2 cup chocolate chips

For the frosting:
- 2/3 cup sugar
- 1/2 cup shortening
- 1/2 cup butter
- 1 teaspoon vanilla
- 2/3 cup evaporated milk

DIRECTIONS

Prepare the dough by beating the cream cheese and butter until creamy. Add the flour and mix thoroughly. Roll into 48 pieces of 1-inch balls, and chill for 2 hours. Place chilled balls in ungreased tassie pans, and press into the sides of the pan. Bake in a 350-degree oven for 15 to 20 minutes. Cool and remove from the pans.

Prepare filling by melting the caramels with the evaporated milk in the microwave until smooth and creamy. Stir in the chocolate chips. Fill the cups with the warm caramel filling, leaving some room for the frosting.

Prepare the frosting by beating the sugar, butter, and shortening until creamy. Add the vanilla. Gradually beat in the evaporated milk, and continue beating until smooth and creamy and, most importantly, the sugar is completely dissolved, about 10 minutes. Fill the tops of each caramel cup with frosting.

CARAMEL OR BUTTERSCOTCH CHIP TOASTED PECAN COOKIES

Sometimes you just need a cookie like a chocolate chip—but not!

INGREDIENTS

5 cups flour
1 teaspoon baking soda
1/2 teaspoon baking powder
3/4 teaspoon salt
1 1/2 cup unsalted butter melted, cooled slightly
1 1/2 cup brown sugar
2 large eggs + 2 egg yolks
1 tablespoon vanilla
1 1/2 cup toasted pecans broken into pieces
2 bags 10 ounce each of caramel or butterscotch chips

DIRECTIONS

Preheat oven to 350 degrees.

Combine the dry ingredients, and set aside.

In a mixer, blend the sugars together. Add the melted butter, and allow to completely mix. Add the eggs and the yolks one at a time and the vanilla. Gradually, add the dry ingredients, and allow this to beat thoroughly.

Stir in by hand the pecans and chips. Shape into balls.

Bake on a greased baking sheet for 12–14 minutes.

CHERRY SURPRISE COOKIES

Cherry surprise cookies are a fun cookie—a nice taste, especially if you enjoy chocolate and cherries together. You might be surprised to learn of some Pittsburgh "firsts." The world's first radio station, KDKA, went on the air in 1920, and the first public television station in the United States, WQED, started broadcasting in 1954. The world's first Ferris wheel was built in 1893 by Pittsburgher George W. Ferris.

INGREDIENTS

1 cup unsalted butter
1/2 cup confectioners' sugar
3/4 teaspoon almond flavoring
2 egg yolks, whisked
1/4 teaspoon salt
2 cups flour, sifted
30 maraschino cherries, rinsed and drained (save the liquid)

DIRECTIONS

Cream the butter and sugar together until fluffy. Add the almond flavoring, egg yolks, and salt, and continue to beat until completely incorporated. Stir in the flour, and mix until a soft dough is formed. Scoop a good teaspoon of dough, and wrap around the maraschino cherry. Place on a greased cookie sheet.

Bake at 325 degrees for 25 minutes or until golden brown. When cooled completely after baking, cookies can be coated in a light icing of 1 1/2 cup powdered sugar combined with 1/4 cup cherry juice.

Options on these cookies include rolling the finished iced cookie in chopped walnuts and/or drizzling chocolate over each cookie.

CHOCOLATE SNOWBALL COOKIES

These are yummy little cookies. The mere image of a snowball makes me smile. You don't even need salt, cinders, or a plow like you would need with snow on the street. Many a youngster in Pittsburgh was able to make some extra money by shoveling driveways and sidewalks. Most of the city sections of Pittsburgh have rules that you must clear your sidewalk of the snow within a certain amount of time. So even to this day, when there is snow, you will see children with shovels in tow, going door-to-door!

INGREDIENTS

1 pound unsalted butter, melted
1 cup cocoa
2 cups sugar
4 teaspoons vanilla extract
1 teaspoon salt
4 cups flour
2 cups walnuts, finely chopped

DIRECTIONS

Cream the butter and sugar together until fluffy.

In a separate bowl, blend together the flour, salt, and cocoa.

Gradually add to the creamed butter and sugar. When combined fully, add the vanilla and then the chopped nuts. Form the dough into a ball, and place in a greased bowl. Cover and refrigerate for 3 to 4 hours.

When chilled, form the dough into 1-inch balls, and bake on an ungreased cookie sheet. Once the cookies are baked, allow to cool, and carefully roll in powdered sugar.

Bake at 350 degrees for 15 minutes.

Yield: 7 dozen.

CHOCOLATE THUMBPRINT COOKIES

Really a beautiful presentation. I make these large for a better effect!

INGREDIENTS

1 1/2 cups butter, softened
2 cups white sugar
6 tablespoons half and half
3 eggs
3 teaspoons vanilla
3 cups all-purpose flour
1 cup cocoa
1/2 teaspoon salt
finely chopped walnuts
2 egg whites, beaten

DIRECTIONS

Beat softened butter until creamy. Add the white sugar, and continue beating. When light and fluffy, beat in the eggs one at a time, half and half, and the vanilla.

In a separate bowl, combine flour, cocoa, and salt. Gradually add it to the butter mixture, and beat. When all ingredients are incorporated, cover and chill for at least 3 hours or overnight.

Shape dough in 1-inch balls, dip into beaten egg white, and roll in nuts. Place on a greased baking sheet. Using your thumb, make an indentation in each ball.

Bake in 350-degree oven for 10–12 minutes.

The filling for the cookie can be icing or a chocolate Kiss. Using a chocolate Kiss, place the Kiss while the cookie is still warm to ensure the Kiss will adhere to the cookie. I love to use fudge icing and pipe a star on each cookie. These freeze very well, and if you freeze them individually first, they can be stored in the freezer without damaging the icing star.

COCONUT MACAROONS

These are a kind of cookie that is easy to make and provides a nice change in texture on a cookie platter.

INGREDIENTS

3 cups coconut
1 cup sweetened condensed milk
1/8 teaspoon salt
1 1/2 teaspoons vanilla
1/2 teaspoon almond
dark chocolate, melted (optional)

DIRECTIONS

Combine all ingredients in a bowl. Drop rounded dollops on to a generously greased cookie sheet.

Bake in a 350-degree oven for 15 minutes or until golden brown.

Cool completely before dipping in chocolate. The bottoms of these macaroons can be dipped in dark chocolate.

CREAM CHEESE WEDDING COOKIES

When putting together a Pittsburgh cookie table, it is important to include a variety of shapes, colors, textures, and styles of cookies. Guests want to enjoy the cookies visually. These simple cream cheese cookies allow the sugar sprinkles on the cookies to match the colors of the bridal party.

INGREDIENTS

8 ounces cream cheese
2 cups shortening
2 cups sugar
5 cups all-purpose flour
2 eggs
1 teaspoon vanilla
sugar sprinkles or turbinado sugar

DIRECTIONS

In a stand mixer, cream the shortening and cream cheese together until very fluffy. Add the sugar, and allow to beat until fully incorporated. Add the eggs, beating in one at a time, and then the vanilla. Reduce the mixer speed, and add the flour in small quantities until the 5 cups are completely mixed into the batter.

Drop 1-inch balls onto an ungreased cookie sheet. Using the bottom of a glass dipped into sugar after each cookie, flatten each cookie, and then sprinkle with your choice of sugars.

Bake at 375 degrees for 15 minutes or until the edges of the cookies are golden.

ITALIAN CHOCOLATE SPICE COOKIES

At our family homestead, the Christmas cookies and treats were put in trays and sitting on the dining room table. My brother, Tom, and I often made our way to the table to steal a cookie or two before our dinner. Although we thought no one knew, I'm sure they all saw us. These were our favorites because of the unique cinnamon-and-chocolate combination. It wasn't quite a chocolate cookie, but it was a really good cookie!

INGREDIENTS

For the cookies:

- 4 cups flour
- 1/2 cup cocoa
- 4 teaspoons baking powder
- 1 teaspoon allspice
- 1/2 teaspoon cloves
- 2 teaspoons cinnamon
- 1 1/2 cups sugar
- 1 cup whole milk
- 1 cup oil
- 1 cup walnuts, chopped
- 1 teaspoon vanilla

For the icing:

- 3/4 cup cocoa
- 4 cups confectioners' sugar
- 1/2 cup butter, melted
- 1 teaspoon vanilla
- 1/2 cup evaporated milk

DIRECTIONS

Blend all the dry ingredients together, and set aside.

Using a mixer, beat the sugar, milk, oil, and vanilla until well blended. Add the dry ingredients gradually. When the dough is mixed, stir in the walnuts. Drop using a teaspoon-sized scoop on to a cookie sheet, and bake.

Bake at 375 degrees for 10–12 minutes.

For the icing, melt butter, and whisk in other ingredients to form smooth icing.

ITALIAN SESAME COOKIES

These cookies are rolled in sesame seeds. You might need to buy a couple jars to have enough to coat each one. They are a simple cookie, great with coffee or tea. They also add a nice texture to a Pittsburgh wedding cookie table.

INGREDIENTS

3 cups flour
1 cups sugar
3 teaspoons baking powder
1/2 teaspoons salt
sesame seeds, toasted
1/2 cup unsalted butter, melted
3 large eggs
3/4 cup whole milk
1 tablespoon vanilla

DIRECTIONS

Cream the butter and sugar together until light and fluffy. Add the eggs one at a time, beating well after each is added. Mix in the vanilla.

In a separate bowl, combine the dry ingredients. Gradually add the dry ingredients to the creamed mixture, and mix well to form a dough. Turn dough out onto a floured surface, and knead 10–12 times. Divide into 8 portions, and shape each portion into a 2-inch diameter log.

Cut each log into 1 1/2-inch pieces. Place the sesame seeds and milk into separate shallow bowls. Roll each piece in milk and then in sesame seeds. Then place the pieces on a greased cookie sheet.

Bake at 350 degrees for 8–10 minutes until bottoms are lightly brown.

KOLACKY COOKIES

This is such a pastry kind of cookie, a delicate dough that is filled with a burst of fruit. The color alone draws your eye, and you just know it is a cookie that needs to be on your plate!

INGREDIENTS

3 ounces cream cheese
1/2 cup unsalted butter, softened
1 cup flour
fruit jam or premade filling
confectioners' sugar

DIRECTIONS

Beat the cream cheese and butter together. Slowly add the flour, and mix until the dough is formed. Shape into a ball, and refrigerate covered overnight.

Working with small amounts of dough, roll out into 1/8-inch thickness, and cut into 2 1/2-inch squares. Place 1/2 teaspoon of filling in the center, fold two opposing corners to the center, and pinch to seal.

Bake on ungreased cookie sheets in a 350-degree oven for 15 minutes. When cool, dust with confectioners' sugar.

LA DOLCHE: ITALIAN WEDDING COOKIES

These cookies are a staple at Italian weddings! A must!

INGREDIENTS

For the cookies:

- 5 cups flour
- 4 tablespoons baking powder
- 1/2 teaspoon salt
- 1/3 cup oil
- 1/4 cup unsalted butter, softened
- 1 cup sugar
- 6 large eggs
- 1 teaspoon lemon extract
- 1 teaspoon anise extract
- 1/2 cup heavy cream

For the glaze:

- 2 cups confectioners' sugar
- 2 teaspoon Vanilla
- 3 tablespoon milk
- dash of lemon extract

DIRECTIONS

In a medium-sized bowl, combine the dry ingredients, and set aside. In a large bowl, blend together the oil and softened butter. Add the sugar to the oil/butter mix, and using a wooden spoon, cream these together. When smooth, add the eggs and flavorings. Once mixed, start adding the dry ingredients alternatively with the heavy cream. If the dough is too moist, an additional 1/2 cup of flour can be added. Cover and refrigerate overnight.

Using floured hands, roll a piece of dough to a 4-inch thin rope. Twist or loosely knot. Place on a lightly greased cookie sheet.

Bake in a 350-degree oven for 12–15 minutes. When cookies are cooled, brush glaze on and sprinkle immediately with colored tiny nonpareil candy balls to match the wedding colors. This makes 5 dozen.

LADY LOCK PASTRY DOUGH

Lady locks are the star of any cookie table. This cookie is not known in many places throughout the United States. I have to make them for Juli's office every time we travel to Florida to visit. They don't know exactly what they are, but they love them!

INGREDIENTS

3 cups flour
2 tablespoons sugar
1/2 teaspoon salt
2 egg yolks
1 cup water
2 cups shortening plus more if needed
small metal dowels or wooden clothes pins (nonclasping)

DIRECTIONS

Lightly beat together the egg yolks and water, and set aside.

In a large bowl, combine the flour, 1/2 cup shortening, egg-yolks-and-water mixture, and sugar until it forms a dough. Divide this dough into three equal parts, and refrigerate for three hours.

Working with the three dough sections separately, roll out each dough into a large rectangle, and spread with a thin layer of shortening. Fold the dough over on itself, and return to the refrigerator for 30 minutes. Repeat this process three times with each of the dough sections.

After the last 30-minute refrigeration, roll your individual sections into a thin rectangle, and cut the rectangle into strips (1 inch by 4–5 inches). Wrap the dough strips around the dowel rods, and place seam side down on a cookie sheet.

Bake in a 400-degree oven for 10 minutes.

Cool completely before filling. This makes 7 dozen.

These cookies freeze very well.

LADY LOCK PASTRY FILLING

Lady locks should have a very silky-smooth pastry cream filling. A stand mixer and patience really help to achieve the right consistency.

INGREDIENTS

1/2 cup unsalted butter, softened
1/2 cup shortening
1 cup sugar
1/2 cup milk
3 tablespoons flour
1 tablespoon vanilla
1 teaspoon lemon juice

DIRECTIONS

Beat the butter and shortening together. Gradually add the sugar, and continue to beat. Once incorporated, add the rest of the ingredients, and allow to beat on high until the sugar is fully dissolved. The filling should be light and fluffy.

Use a piping bag to fill the lady lock pastries.

LIZ'S SUGARED COOKIE FINGERS

Everyone has a best friend… Liz, my angel in heaven!

INGREDIENTS

1 2/3 cup flour
2 teaspoons baking powder
1/2 teaspoon salt
1/2 teaspoon almond or vanilla extract
1 3/4 cup powdered sugar
1 egg
1/2 cup unsalted butter

DIRECTIONS

Sift together the flour, baking powder, and salt. Add the butter, powdered sugar, egg, and flavoring to the flour mix. Beat until smooth. Chill the dough for several hours or overnight.

Roll dough, and form into 3-by-4-inch logs.

Bake in a 375-degree oven for 8 minutes.

MINATURE CHEESECAKES

Baby cheesecakes—really, how great is that! Small package, big taste. It is everything that is good in life and more!

INGREDIENTS

2 8-ounce packages of cream cheese, softened
3/4 cup sugar
1 tablespoon lemon juice
2 large eggs
1 teaspoon vanilla
vanilla wafer cookies

DIRECTIONS

Beat the softened cream cheese in a mixing bowl, and add the sugar. Beat until creamy and smooth. Beat in the eggs one at a time. Add in the vanilla and lemon juice. Beat until the mix is very smooth, about 5 to 7 minutes. Set this aside.

In a tassie pan, place a small vanilla wafer in each cup. It is optional if you would like to use a paper liner for each cookie. Place about a tablespoon of filling in each cup.

Bake in a 350-degree oven for 15 minutes. Tiny cracks may appear on the top of each cookie.

These cheesecakes can be served plain or with a fruit pie filling topping.

NUT HORNS

So worth the effort! The sugary fluffy egg white nut mix will gently ooze out the sides. This is a very delicate pastry with a soothing sweet-nut flavor.

INGREDIENTS

For the pastry:

- 4 cups flour
- 1 teaspoon salt
- 1 cake of yeast
- 1 1/4 cup unsalted butter
- 1/2 cup sour cream
- 5 egg yolks
- 1 teaspoon vanilla

For the filling:

- 5 egg whites
- 1 cup sugar
- 1 teaspoon vanilla
- 1/2 teaspoon almond extract
- 1 cup ground walnut meat

DIRECTIONS

Sift the flour and salt together. Allow the butter and yeast to soften to room temperature. Add to the flour, and use a pastry blender until the mix resembles cornmeal. Combine the sour cream and egg yolks, and add to the flour mix. Mix and pull the dough together with a fork like a pie crust. Divide the dough into 6 portions. Roll each portion into a 9-inch round.

For the filling, beat the egg whites until very stiff. Add the sugar gradually while beating. Carefully fold in the vanilla, almond extracts, and nut meat.

Once you have made the filling, divide it into 9 portions. Spread on each dough circle, and cut into 12 pie wedges. Roll from the outside edge to the center. Place on cookie sheet point down, and bake immediately.

Bake in a 325-degree oven for 30 minutes.

PEACH COOKIES

These are a must for every wedding cookie table! There is no need to have hundreds of cookies; a nice tray with a couple dozen peach cookies make for a beautiful spread. They are also a perfect accent on a tray of a mixed variety of cookies. They tend to be somewhat larger than other cookies, and the peach color is eclectic and striking.

INGREDIENTS

For the cookies:

- 4 large eggs
- 1 cup sugar
- 1 cup oil
- 1–2 large packages of peach-flavored gelatin
- 4 cups flour
- 3 teaspoons baking powder
- 1/2 cup peach schnapps

For the filling:

- 5 tablespoons flour
- 1 cup milk
- 1/2 cup butter
- 1/2 cup shortening
- 1 cup confectioners' sugar
- 1 teaspoon vanilla

DIRECTIONS

Beat the eggs slightly, then add in order: sugar, oil, flour, and baking powder. Combine well. Chill for 1 hour. Roll into small balls, and bake on a cookie sheet.

Bake in a 375-degree oven for 10 minutes. Allow to cool, and scoop out a little from the underside of each cookie.

Prepare the filling by mixing the flour and milk in a saucepan. Cook over low heat until it becomes thick. Place in a bowl, and set aside.

Cream together the butter and shortening, and add the confectioners' sugar. When fully mixed, add the flour-and-milk mix and vanilla. Continue to beat until fluffy.

Put a small amount of filling in the scooped-out opening on the underside of 2 cookies, and put together as a sandwich cookie.

Combine 1/2 cup peach schnapps with red food coloring, and put it in a shallow bowl. Roll each cookie in the peach schnapps and into the peach gelatin. Add a green plastic stem or pipe green icing to resemble a stem.

PEANUT BUTTER BLOSSOMS

Peanut butter blossoms are a unique treat, especially because there is a chocolate Kiss waiting for you at the top of each cookie! The question remains, Which do you eat first, the cookie or the Kiss? The answer—*both*!

INGREDIENTS

- 1 cup shortening
- 1 cup brown sugar, packed
- 2 large eggs
- 2 teaspoons vanilla
- 2 teaspoons baking soda
- 2 9-ounce bags chocolate Kisses, unwrapped
- Additional granulated sugar for rolling
- 1 cup peanut butter
- 1 cup white sugar
- 1/4 cup milk
- 3 1/2 cups flour
- 1/2 teaspoon salt

DIRECTIONS

In a medium bowl, mix together the dry ingredients, and set aside.

In a large bowl, cream together the shortening, peanut butter, and brown and white sugar until smooth and creamy. Beat in the eggs one at a time. When incorporated, beat in the milk and vanilla. Blend in the dry ingredients to form a dough.

Using a 1-inch cookie scoop, roll each ball in granulated sugar, and place on a greased cookie sheet.

Bake in a 375-degree oven for 10–12 minutes. Unwrap the Kisses. When the cookies come out of the oven, press 1 Kiss onto the top of each cookie immediately. Allow to set and cool.

PEANUT BUTTER BUCKEYES

Gooey sweet peanut butter surrounded by a rich chocolate coating—one of those special one-bite cookies that just call your name and then say, "Hey, where's the cold milk?"

INGREDIENTS

1/2 cup unsalted butter
1 pound confectioners' sugar
1 1/2 teaspoons vanilla
1 1/2 cups creamy peanut butter
coating chocolate

DIRECTIONS

Cream together the butter and sugar until smooth. Add the peanut butter and vanilla. Beat until creamy.

Using a cookie scoop, shape into balls. Place on a cookie sheet, and refrigerate for two hours.

Insert a toothpick in the top of each ball to allow you to dip the ball into the melted chocolate. Coat each ball about 3/4 of the way up the ball. The cookie should then resemble a "buckeye."

Place on a cookie sheet covered in wax paper. Allow these cookies to chill until firm.

PECAN TASSIE COOKIES

Pecan pie in a cookie—delicious just doesn't quite describe it! It's like putting a piece of the South in your mouth!

INGREDIENTS

For the dough:

6 ounces cream cheese, softened
3/4 cup unsalted butter, softened
2 cups flour

For the filling:

1 large egg
3/4 cup packed brown sugar
1 teaspoon vanilla
1 tablespoon butter, melted
1/2 cup pecans, finely chopped

DIRECTIONS

Cream together the butter and cream cheese. Add the flour, beating until a dough forms. Refrigerate the dough for an hour. In a separate bowl, whisk together the egg, melted butter, vanilla, brown sugar, and pecans. Set the filling aside. Form the dough into 1-inch balls, and shape into the cups of a tassie pan. Fill each cup with the pecan filling.

Bake in a 325-degree oven for 25 minutes or until the filling is set. Allow cookies to cool.

This makes 36 cookies.

PIGNOLI COOKIES

A special cookie that may cost a little more than the average. Every visit to the Italian Bakery always ends with a few of these in your bag.

INGREDIENTS

- 8–9 ounces (1 cup) marzipan
- 1/4 cup sugar
- 1/8 teaspoon salt
- 2–3 drops bitter almond oil
- 2–3 drops lemon oil
- 1/2 cup almond flour
- 1 egg white
- 1 1/2 cups pine nuts

DIRECTIONS

Break up the marzipan in pieces into a medium-sized bowl. Mix in the sugar, salt, flavoring oils, and almond flour. Mix until crumbly. Add the egg white, and beat until the mixture is smooth. Place the pine nuts in a shallow dish.

Using a 1-teaspoon cookie scoop, drop doughballs into the pine nuts, and roll, allowing the cookie to be coated with nuts. Place on a lightly greased cookie sheet or parchment.

Bake in a 325-degree oven for 22–24 minutes or until lightly browned. Cool and store in an airtight container, or these cookies can be frozen.

This makes 3 dozen.

PIZZELLES

This is my mom's pizzelle recipe—tried and true. You can eat them like the delicate cookie that they are. You can roll them and fill them. You can make a bowl and fill it with ice cream. Any way you eat them, they're a traditional Pittsburgh treat!

INGREDIENTS

12 large eggs
3 cups white granulated sugar
2 cups butter, melted and cooled
1/4 cup vanilla (2 teaspoons of anise can be substituted)
7 cups flour
2 tablespoons plus 2 teaspoons baking powder

DIRECTIONS

Beat eggs and sugar until fluffy. Stir in the cooled melted butter.

In a separate bowl, mix the flour and baking powder together. Mix the dry ingredients into the eggs and sugar. Add the vanilla or anise, and mix well. The batter will be sticky.

Heat a pizzelle iron, and lightly grease the surfaces. Drop batter by teaspoon (you can use a cookie scoop), and bake until golden. If you are rolling or molding the pizzelles, it must be done right off the grill while the cookies are still hot and pliable.

RUSSIAN TEA CAKES

These resemble white snowballs. They are rich in a buttery goodness that pair well with the walnuts. A very well-liked cookie not only at weddings but also at Christmas! A versatile and useful cookie, quick and easy to make.

INGREDIENTS

1 cup unsalted butter, softened
1/2 cup confectioners' sugar
1 teaspoon vanilla
1 3/4 cup flour
1/2 cup walnuts, chopped
additional confectioners' sugar

DIRECTIONS

Cream together the butter and sugar until smooth. Add the vanilla, flour, and nuts, and mix to form a dough.

Using a 1-inch cookie scoop, drop balls on an ungreased cookie sheet.

Bake in a 350-degree oven for 18–20 minutes.

Roll each baked and slightly cooled cookie in confectioners' sugar.

These cookies freeze very well.

RASPBERRY SHORTBREAD THUMBPRINTS

Thumbprint cookies of any kind are always welcome on a cookie table! They add a nice touch of color to the arrangement. The jam you choose for this cookie is really up to you, the baker.

INGREDIENTS

For the cookies:

- 1 cup butter, softened
- 2/3 cup granulated sugar
- 1 teaspoon vanilla
- 2 cups flour
- 1/2 cup seedless raspberry jam

For the icing:

- 1/2 cup confectioners' sugar
- 3/4 teaspoon vanilla
- 1 teaspoon milk

DIRECTIONS

Cream together the butter and granulated sugar until smooth. Add the vanilla. Mix in the flour until a dough is formed. Roll the dough into 1 1/2-inch balls and place on an ungreased cookie sheet. Using your thumb make an indentation in each cookie. Fill the indentation with the jam.

Bake in a 350-degree oven for 15–18 minutes or until golden. Remove from the oven and allow to cool.

Mix together the confectioners' sugar, 3/4 teaspoon vanilla and one teaspoon milk to form an icing. Drizzle over each cookie.

This makes 3 dozen cookies.

SNICKERDOODLES

Snickerdoodles are a fun cinnamon cookie that are very easy to make and even easier to eat. They are homey, and pair warmly with a cup of hot chocolate, tea, or coffee. It's nice to add a cinnamon cookie to your cookie table display. Variety is the "cinnamon" spice of life!

INGREDIENTS

- 1/2 cup shortening
- 1 1/2 cup sugar
- 2 3/4 cup flour
- 1 teaspoon baking soda
- 3 tablespoons sugar plus 3 teaspoons cinnamon
- 1/2 cup unsalted butter
- 2 large eggs, beaten
- 2 teaspoons cream of tartar
- 1/4 teaspoon salt

DIRECTIONS

In a medium bowl, combine the dry ingredients, and set aside.

Cream together the shortening and butter. Add in the sugar, and continue to beat until very smooth. Add in the eggs one at a time. With your mixer on low speed, gradually add the dry ingredients to form a dough. Shape into 1-inch balls, and roll in the sugar-and-cinnamon mixture.

Bake in a 400-degree oven on ungreased cookie sheets for 8–10 minutes.

THUMBPRINTS WITH ICING

This cookie is the thumbprint many people use at weddings because the icing can be tinted to match the color theme of the wedding.

INGREDIENTS

1 cup butter, softened
1/2 cup brown sugar
2 eggs, separate the yolks and whites
2 cups flour
1 teaspoon vanilla
1/2 teaspoon salt
1 cup ground walnuts

DIRECTIONS

Cream together the butter and brown sugar. Add the egg yolks one at a time and then the vanilla, and continue to beat until light and fluffy. Sift and flour and salt in a separate bowl.

In small increments, add the flour to the butter mixture. Form dough into balls, dip into the beaten egg whites, and roll in ground nuts.

Make a imprint with your thumb. (You may have to redo the thumbprint immediately after removing from the oven.)

Bake in a 375-degree oven for 12–14 minutes.

When cooled, fill with colored icing.

TRUDY'S CHOCOLATE CHIP COOKIES

I could not ask for a better neighbor and friend than Trudy! She is like a sister to me, and she is known for these yummy cookies. We have been known to get into predicaments. When I was head of the drama guild at the school, it was my job to pick up the explosives we used during the shows. Trudy volunteered to go with me. Convinced that we were going to explode on the way home, we doused the entire car and ourselves with antistatic spray and drove in the snow with the windows down just to be sure we would be safe. Truth is, I am pretty sure the assistant director might have been yanking our chains, but better safe than sorry! And we made it home safely without exploding!

INGREDIENTS

1 3/4 cup flour (add 1/2 cup more flour to raise cookies)
1 teaspoon salt
1 teaspoon baking soda
1 1/4 cup brown sugar
3/4 cup butter-flavored shortening
2 tablespoons whole milk
1 tablespoon vanilla
1 egg
1 bag 10-ounce semisweet chocolate chips

DIRECTIONS

Mix the dry ingredients together, and set aside.

Cream the shortening and brown sugar together until very smooth and fluffy. Into the creamed mixture, add the egg. Mix well, and add the milk and vanilla. Beat until incorporated, and gradually then add the flour mixture. Stir in the bag of chocolate chips.

Bake at 375 degrees for 10 to 12 minutes.

WHIPPED SHORTBREAD

These cookies are a delicate shortbread. They have a rich flavor for such an unassuming cookie!

INGREDIENTS

1 cup unsalted butter
1 1/2 cup flour
1/2 cup confectioners' sugar
1 teaspoon vanilla

DIRECTIONS

Combine all ingredients, and whip in a stand mixer for at least ten minutes. Drop by teaspoons onto baking sheet. Decorate each cookie top with either an almond or half of a green or red cherry, and bake.

Bake at 325 degrees for 12–15 minutes until the edges are slightly golden. Let cool on the cookie sheet for 5 minutes before removing.

EXTRA COOKING TIPS

The following are general rules for cooking and baking.

When baking, be exact in following recipes. A recipe is like a scientific formula.

When cooking, follow the recipe, but you have some flexibility, so you can alter to your likes, dislikes, and tastes.

Whether baking or cooking, read your recipe at least twice before you start.

Set your ingredients out—even premeasure them if you like. Be aware that distractions (like talking on the phone, texting, etc.) can lead to an unfortunate mistake that could alter the quality of your dish.

If you need buttermilk and have none, place 1 tablespoon of white vinegar in a 1-cup measuring cup. Add milk to the 1 cup line, and allow to sit for 5 minutes at room temperature. It will transform into a buttermilk substitute.

Raisins are great but can be quite hard and difficult to bake with. Plumping raisins before baking is a must. Measure your raisins, and cover with boiling water or heated liquid, such as juice, wine, brandy, or rum. Drain when the desired consistency is met. Happy baking!

Always allow eggs to come to room temperature before adding to your baking recipes.

When it comes to flour and baking, be very careful of how the recipe is written. Recipes that call for "1 cup sifted flour" means you sift the flour and then measure. Recipes that call for "1 cup flour, sifted" means you should measure the flour then sift.

When measuring corn syrup, honey, or molasses, spray the measuring cup with a cooking spray first. This will allow for easy removal.

Cake batters—they are all not alike! Those batters made with whipped egg whites that are folded into the batter should only be shaken before baking. Tapping these pans will undo the efforts of your egg whites. Batters with whole eggs can be tapped to remove bubbles.

Egg wash is a wonderful finishing for a pastry. Whisk together a large egg and one tablespoon of water. Brush on pastries for a golden finish. It can also be used for sealing pastry sides together.

Oven temperatures can vary. Most grocery stores sell small metal stand-up thermometers that you can place in your oven to make sure you are using the correct temperature when baking.

Little things can change your cooking/baking success:

- Dry your meat before you cook it.
- Toast your nuts before you use them.
- Cut your coconut into smaller strands for your baking needs.
- Don't use dried out coconut; rehydrate in a tad of milk.

- Don't be afraid to season; bland anything is a food crime. Salt is good, and so is sugar! Sugar especially enhances the flavor of tomatoes.
- Never crowd a pan. Allow for things to be heated on all sides.
- Always save some of your pasta water for your sauce. It can add great flavor and will help with the consistency.
- Broth is made from the actual meat.
- Stock is made from the bones and trimmings of the meat.
- Some dishes need a drizzle of olive oil for the finishing touch. Pasta, pizza, and some meats can benefit from a little olive oil on top!
- If you cannot find shallots, use some garlic *and* onion. A shallot is both!
- When frying or sautéing, never put your product in cold oil. Test with a small piece, and make sure the oil bubbles before you start. This tells you that it is hot enough to cook properly.
- Eggs—cook them slow on low. And when you need them, crack them in a dish first in case you get shells or the egg is bad.

ACKNOWLEDGMENTS

Les Niehl

Thanks to my husband. Without his love and support, unending patience, and encouragement, this effort would not have come to fruition. I have loved every minute working with you. Thank you for spending hours getting this book organized and edited. You are such a gift to me, and I truly adore you. Now it's your turn to write!

Jake Niehl

Thanks to my son Jake for being my creative go to. Your patience and honesty were so appreciated. You were always willing to listen to my ideas, and I relied on your input more times than you know. Your cover design is perfect. Thank you for your love and support. Love you, Jake!

Adam Niehl

Thanks to Adam for being my "foodie." You are always willing to push my culinary boundaries as no other. Your food knowledge and ability are top notch and really can get me excited over trying things I didn't even know how to cook, like that pork belly. Thanks for chairing the "foreword committee.". I appreciate you for always encouraging me to forge onward and upward. Love you, Bud!

Julia Niehl

Thanks to my daughter, Julia, my cheerleader. Despite being a thousand miles away, you were trying recipes, reviewing photos, and offering all the support you could. I know one day your cooking prowess will far exceed mine. Jul, you are my sunshine, and I love you!

Cathy May

Thanks for being the sister I've never had. We have been through so much. Obviously, Mom liked you best. We always had to have corn for you at family dinners. And of course, my parents loved those damn picnic rolls more than anything. Please know I appreciate your daily encouragement and I am so glad we are family!

Suzy Bujakowski

Thanks to my very special cousin. We are family first and always. Thanks for helping me with the ethnic recipes and remembering the old times in Braddock. I love our escapades, laughs, and watching our kids grow.

Trudy Hoover

Thanks to my walking buddy who put up with miles of cookbook talk. You were always the springboard for my culinary ideas and offered a ton of positive feedback. Always know that you are an excellent cook and your willingness to explore new recipes and techniques truly inspire me.

Lynn Palmer

You are my BFF, friend to the end. Thanks for always encouraging me and always being so positive about this cookbook. I have no doubt that you will have the first copy off the press! I appreciate your support and friendship.

Brooks Bratten

Thanks to our unofficial son, Brooks, for being the one professional journalist and great "foodie." You were there to encourage me when I questioned my efforts. Despite your very busy schedule, you always made time to answer my calls and text messages.

ABOUT THE AUTHOR

Joanne Lutton Niehl is most at home in her kitchen. She was born and raised in Pittsburgh, and her fondest memories involve cooking, hosting gatherings, and enjoying meals with family and friends. Jo graduated from the University of Pittsburgh and had a career working as a legislative assistant for the Pennsylvania House of Representatives. She married Les Niehl and left her career to be a full-time mom to her children—Jacob, Adam, and Julia.

Jo has always volunteered in her children's schools. Over the span of many years, she coordinated a reading program in the kids' elementary school, became an aide to special-needs students, and was president of the high school parent drama guild. But her most gratifying volunteer effort was operating the two stadium food stands during high school football games that benefited the marching band. Pittsburgh loves their Friday night high school football, and they love their food, which was the perfect setting for Jo and Les to host their biggest parties ever. Band parents were on a waiting list to volunteer; the concession stand was the place to be on Friday night!

After the kids moved on, Joanne continued her cooking and baking, including specialty birthday cakes and award-winning gingerbread houses. The kitchen is always open in her home, and there is always a chair for you!

CPSIA information can be obtained
at www.ICGtesting.com
Printed in the USA
BVHW021835091122
651605BV00004B/13